Career Planning & Development

Preparation – Planning - Performance

15 Easy Ways to Start a New Career or Grow Your Existing One!

By

The Customer Service Training Institute

Other Training Manuals from The Customer Service Training Institute

Customer Service Basics

Conflict Resolution

Service Recovery Skills

How to Interact with All Kinds of Customers

Great Customer Service Over the Phone

Customer Service for Frontline Personnel

Enhancing the Customer Experience

Customer Service Training for
Service Technicians

Customer Service Training for
the Hospitality Sector

Customer Service Training for
Health Care Professionals

Customer Service Excellence for
Security Officers

Safety in the Workplace

Office Skills Training Series

Dealing with Difficult People

"If you do not change anything, nothing will change. YOU have to take control of your own future and destiny!"

Disclaimer

This publication is intended to be used as a resource only and it not intended to be used as a self contained plan for any one individual. Some or all of the content in this publication may not be appropriate for any situation or application. It is the sole responsibility of the reader to determine the suitability of any or all parts of this book. We urge anyone reading this book to carefully consider the suitability of any part before implementing it in their lives.

Contents

Introduction

When it comes to careers, one thing is almost always true. We almost never end our career with the same job we started it with. Over time, we change jobs to fit our skills, experience and overall goals. We may switch industries or positions within the same industry. But we rarely stay still or remain in the same place.

There are a lot of ways in which we can advance or build a career. Since everyone is different and every situation is different as well, it is not possible to have one perfect master plan or blueprint to follow when it comes to growing our own career.

That's the bad news but the good news is that there are many different ways an individual can grow his or her own career that do not take a lot of effort or resources. In fact, the great news is that often all that is required to take one's career to the next level and beyond is a simple attitude adjustment.

By attitude adjustment we mean looking at something differently. We mean changing the way we act or react to a certain situation, problem or even opportunity. When we change the way we see things, we often change our actions and reactions as well. As in most things in life, when we change our actions or reactions, we also change the results.

Throughout this book we are going to challenge the way you look at things associated with your job, career and sometimes your life. We are going to talk about how these things influence your ability to grow your career, increase the level of success in your life and several other things.

As we do this, we ask two things of you. First, read through the entire book. Even though you might not think something applies to you or your situation, read it anyway. You never know when you might realize that something is different than you always thought it was!

The second thing is to have an open mind as you read through the different topics and suggestions contained in the book. Everything in this book was carefully chosen because it is important as far as careers and advancement is concerned. Just because you might think you disagree with what we say, be open to a different view and how it might help you moving forward.

Always keep in mind that the goal is not to be right or wrong, just to get the results you are looking for.

You might also see a few things repeated more than once during the course of this book. This is not to make the book longer but instead we do that for two very important reasons. First, some people like to skip around or go directly to the parts of a book that they feel they have an immediate need for. In those cases we want to make sure you have the information you need to completely understand what you are reading. So we will provide all the information and background needed for complete understanding.

Second, sometimes a certain topic or concept might apply to more than one issue or situation. When that occurs we will discuss the same topic or concept although from a different perspective or viewpoint. This not only helps bring things into better focus, the repeating of such critical information helps the reader retain the materials in their brains for longer periods of time.

Last, but certainly not least, reading through this book should not become a contest to see how fast you can get through it. We have done our best to bring the important information to you in a short and concise manner so that you can get results faster. So this book is not some 500 page volume that will take you weeks to get through.

Instead, take your time and really understand what you are reading. One of the best ways to not only understand but remember something is to take the information off the pages you read and think about how to bring that information into your own individual situation. Not only does this help you understand, it makes the information relevant and that will help you retain it longer.

One of the reasons why we were so excited during the design and writing of this book was because the information contained in these pages will help you in other areas of your life as well. So the approaches and attitudes described here will help you much more than growing your career or getting a new job.

So grab yourself something to drink, find a quiet spot and let's get started!

You Deserve the Best You are Capable Of!

No career guide or job hunting manual would be complete if it doesn't cover the psychological aspects of the process. While you might not realize it, many people sabotage their efforts because they feel that somehow they either don't deserve success or that they are not skilled enough to do better in life than they are already doing.

I want to tell you right now that you DO deserve to have the best in life that you are capable of. You DESERVE to accomplish things in life that are within your skills and abilities. To expect anything less is to do a disservice to you and your family. You should always push yourself to put forth the best effort and to produce the very best results.

Also please note that I am not saying anyone is "entitled" to success or money or anything as far as their careers are concerned. While everyone should have the same rights as everyone else, we need to understand that we should expect results based on our efforts and skills. We should not expect to be handed things in life because it doesn't work that way. If we see something we want, we need to figure out a way to work towards that in life. We should not expect it to be handed to us with little or no effort.

The good news is that if we understand that we need to hold ourselves to a higher standard than others might, we will find ourselves outperforming most other people. Part of this entails creating a new attitude and accepting accountability.

Accountability means taking responsibility and being accountable for the things we do in life. When we accept responsibility we tend to apply ourselves more and make more progress. If we blame others then we rarely will move forward.

As we start the process, make a commitment to yourself to do the very best you can and to take advantage of the resources available to you life. You don't have to be the expert if you have access to one! If you cannot create a nice looking resume, then find someone who can help you. If you can't write a cover letter, ask someone who can. Don't let pride get in the way.

Tell yourself you deserve success and that you are entitled for a shot at it. Don't tell yourself that you are not worthy because you are. Don't convince yourself that you have no chance because you do. If you never take the first step you will never move from where you are.

It is all right to take a first step and fail or fall. When that happens, and it does to the best of us, pick yourself up, learn from your mistake, and do things differently next time. Because every time we do something or every time we experience something and learn from it we become stronger, more powerful and more qualified.

There is only one way you can let yourself down in life and that is by not giving your best effort. Just remember that you can do this, you should always do your best and that you should always move on. Keep a positive attitude towards life and your career and you will find opportunities and success coming your way even when you are not pursuing it.

Just do your best and some things just take care of themselves!

Attitude

How we approach certain things has a direct influence on just how successful we are going to be. Our attitude also influences the quality of our work, the amount of effort we put into something and how productive we are as well. A strong case can be made that your attitude is one of the most important determining factors in our success or failure. You will notice that we talk about this subject throughout the book at different points. That is because it is so important and relevant to what we are doing.

When it comes to attitude, you need to consider at least two important factors. Those factors are relevance and importance. How we view each of these will have a direct impact on the attitude we develop towards something.

It is important that we understand the relevance of something because when we understand what something really is and how we will be affected by it; our attitude towards it will change. Think about the times when you were asked to do something that you felt there was no benefit in it for you. Perhaps it was being asked to learn a foreign language in High School or Calculus in college. If you saw no benefit in doing that, you likely didn't put your best effort into it. That is just human nature.

But if you are supposed to do something that you feel is very relevant to whom you are or what you want to accomplish, you will have a much more positive attitude and you will put forth a better and more sustained effort. When you understand why something is relevant to you it is much easier to stay focused and motive. It is also much harder to get distracted as well!

As far as our career and job hunting is concerned, it is important to understand that EVERY part of the process is DIRECTLY relevant to our success in getting a new or better job. No one part of the process is unimportant. The entire process is designed to flow from one step to the next. If the process is interrupted at any point, the job goes to someone else!

So if you think a cover letter is not worth your time, think again. If you feel you it is not important to prepare yourself for an interview or position yourself for the best chances of success, then think again.

Every part of the process is relevant to your success!

Importance is another area where we should understand what we will actually gain from doing a particular task or when we achieve a certain goal. This is the "What's in it for me?" part of the equation. This is where the most powerful motivation often comes from.

In order to convince our brains that something is important, it helps to think about or write down what the benefits might be if we are successful. IN the case of getting a new or better job, what might the benefits be for you if you are successful and get that new job?

You might make more money and that would enable you to buy a house or a new car. That could easily be seen as a benefit. You might be able to start a family or go on a nice vacation once a year. You might be able to finally get out of debt as well. All those things are benefits.

There are other benefits other than money as well. You might get more job security or finally being able to break through into a new position or career that you always wanted. A benefit might be something as innocent as seeing more possibilities and opportunities ahead for you in the future.

Whatever might be better, easier, or benefit you if you are successful should be written down and thought about throughout the process.

This will help you become more committed and more focused because you see why you are doing what you are doing and how life will be better once you are successful. This can be one of the most powerful motivators you can have in your life!

One More Attitude Adjustment

You will also see several references to being "good enough" to be able to do something or qualify for something. A lot of people look at things and say to themselves "OK, this should be good enough to get me an interview" or "This should be good enough to get me a job offer." If you have this particular attitude, you might be standing between you and success.

Striving to be "good enough" is often not going to be "good enough". Remember that getting a job offer is a competitive process. You will be going up against tens or hundreds of other people who are also trying to look their best and land that job. They might all be good enough to get the job so you have to be better in order to stand out from the rest.

That is why you need to develop the attitude that you are going to do your very best to be the best and produce the best at every step of the process. That means creating the very best resume and cover letter. It means doing your very best to ace every job interview.

Last, but certainly not least, it is about doing what it takes to put yourself in the best possible position to land that job.

It should be your attitude to create an overall impression that makes people feel that they HAVE to hire you not that they could hire you. You want whoever is in charge of hiring to think only about you and no one else. In other words, you should try and be on a higher level than everyone else. Let those who are good enough look for another job where they are good enough. That might be OK for them but not for you.

This attitude also has to translate into interviews as well. Your goal should not be to convince someone that you are qualified for the job. Your resume and cover letter probably already have established that. IN an interview it should be your goal to convince the interviewer that you are the MOST qualified. You want other people to fall to the side as you continue to impress the interviewer about you and your qualifications.

We will talk about "connecting the dots" later on in this book. That means making sure that every step of the process is controlled and defined by YOUR efforts. Leave nothing to chance. Do not assume someone knows something that they might not know. Lead the interviewer down the road you want to do so that everything that is said and discussed makes you out to be the best candidate for the job.

If you fail to do your best at any one step in the process, you might not make it to the next step. If you are great during an interview but you put together a lousy resume, you might not even make it to the interview. If you fail to do the right amount of preparation in the beginning, you might not even make it to getting your resume even considered!

Don't tell yourself something is good enough if you can do better. You don't have to be perfect but you should try to be. Your attitude should be to create the very best impression you possibly can. If you do that and you lose, then so be it. There will be more opportunities heading your way.

But if you convince yourself that being "good enough" is good enough for you, then be prepared to stay right where you are because others with the right attitude are going to pass you by.

If all of this sounds depressing or scary, that is not our intention. The good news is that there are a ton of people applying for the jobs you are applying for who feel that good enough is just fine. That is great for you because you will rise above all of them! It is not hard and there are no special skills required to make yourself better! You can just refuse to do less than your best and you will do just fine.

And that should be more than good enough!

Social Media,

the Internet & You

No book about careers and job hunting would be complete today without a discussion of social media and its influence in your life and career. Social Media is a force that needs to be understood and reckoned with. While some of our younger readers might think this chapter was written by some old fart with no idea how the modern world operates, let me say that every single thought represented in this chapter is 100% true. It has not been overstated, blown out of proportion or fabricated in any way shape or form.

So please read this with an open mind and think very carefully about the content in this chapter. We saved it until last for a reason. This is something we want to have fresh in everyone's mind whether you are starting your career or trying to grow and build your existing one. So please, read on and think about this carefully.

The world has changed considerably since I went out on my first job interview. In those "old days" you could get away with certain things and even make a mistake or two and learn from them without doing yourself too much harm.

Today everything is different.

Everyone today has a cell phone camera and everyone today is connected in some way to the internet. This means information and pictures that may include you could wind up anywhere at any time with or without your knowledge. Friends could put pictures on their FaceBook page or mention you in a post and that would be put out there for everyone to see!

You might ask why that might be such a big deal. Well background checks and pre-employment screenings usually include some kind of internet checks as well. Prospective hires are likely to have their names run through a series of name checks to see what content might show up. They are not searching for anything specifically (they will also do criminal and DMV checks, though) they are just seeing what pops up when they type your name into Google and other search engines.

So it is important that you manage your presence or "footprint" on the internet as closely and carefully as you can.

The last thing you want is for the interviewer, or other Human Resource person, to search and find lewd pictures or inappropriate comments about you during their search. This could derail even the most qualified candidate's efforts.

Here are a few things to consider when it comes to your own presence on the Internet:

It's Easy to Share!

When it comes to the Internet, one overlying truth is that it is easy to share pictures, information and data with other people. You don't have to talk to anyone, you can do this anonymously or through a false name and there is no one to question you about authenticity when you do it.

This makes it easy for cowards and people with hidden agendas to spread rumors and untruths about other people. It makes it just as easy to damage someone's reputation as it is to strengthen it or make it better.

Because it is so easy, and because there will always be a group of people with warped ideals and a sick sense of humor, we must always remain aware and on-guard when it comes to how we are portrayed on the Internet.

Be Careful with Social Media

It never ceases to amaze me the things people post on the various Social Media sites. They give personal details about themselves, let people know where they are and what they are doing and just share way too much about their personal lives in what amounts to a public forum.

Do you realize when you put it on Social Media that you are out of town that you are making it easy for people to know when your house is empty and a great target for a robbery? Don't give me all that garbage about only your friends being able to see what you post. People have a way of seeing everything when they really want to. Plus, word of mouth, someone looking over your friend's shoulders while they read and other methods do not make your entries private or secure at all!

But also keep in mind that everything you place on FaceBook or other sites is out there forever. If you share unflattering photographs of yourself, they will be out there forever. And you also have little control over what other people might do with those photographs. Copy and paste is a powerful tool when used in the wrong hands!

Protect Your Identity

By now I am sure you have heard about identity theft and possibly even known someone who had his or her identity stolen by someone else.

That can be very serious and result in lost money, damaged reputations and other issues. People have damaged credit ratings (something some employers also check), comments posted in their name that they did not make and other issues.

Do not share your personal information over the internet for any reason. Items like your Social Security number and other personal data should be kept private except for uses and sites that you are 100% positive and legitimate.

Before you post anything online, whether it is personal information on yourself or details about what you are doing or where you are going, make sure you really need and want to do that. If there is any doubt, delete what you are writing and don't post it.

Check Those URL's!

One common way people get information from unsuspecting people is by creating "look alike" sites that look exactly like the real and legitimate site but whose purpose is strictly to get you name, account numbers, passwords and any other personal information they need to take whatever is yours.

For example, you might get an e-mail from someone representing themselves as your bank asking you to "verify" your account information.

The site looks just like your real bank site and they ask you to enter your account number and password or pin number. But that information goes to another site and once they have it, they move you money from your account to theirs and it's gone! That is just one example but there are many designed to get personal information about you that they can use against you.

The smart thing to do is to look carefully at the URL of the link. If it is not EXACTLY like the real bank link, do not use that link. A name might be very close and appear misspelled or have extra characters in it or something along those lines. One common one is an e-mail supposedly coming from "PayPal" but the link is for a site named "PeyPal". Close but not the real link.

If you have any doubt whether or not the link is legitimate, contact support FROM THE REAL WEBSITE NOT FROM THE LINK IN THE EMAIL and confirm the request.

We are telling you all of this to help you protect your identity and not become a victim who will have credit problems and other problems that may show up on an employer's screening and ruin your chances for a job!

Check Your Credit Rating!

Employers will check credit ratings to get an idea of how well you manage your money and what your attitude towards credit is.

They do this to make sure you do not have money problems that might influence your ability to do your best at your job. They also do not want people with poor money management skills to be placed in a position to handle money either!

But a more important reason to check your credit report is that there might be false information contained in your report that is damaging your reputation. Errors can always be made and you should not suffer from those errors. Checking your report 3 or 4 times a year will enable you to watch out for those types of errors and keep your record clean.

Another reason is one that we already discussed and that is identity theft. If you check your report and you see bank accounts and credit card accounts that are not yours, then you might be a victim of identity theft. By checking your report you can contact the credit card companies and financial institutions and make them aware of the problems. It might be a simple mistake like someone with your exact name and a similar Social Security number or it could be identity theft. You want to uncover these things as quickly as possible to minimize the damage and preserve your credit rating.

There are several internet sites that will provide you with free credit report information. But before you give anyone your personal data or information, do a search to make sure these sites are legitimate and not scams themselves!

Do Frequent Searches

As we have said, much of what you may find on the internet is out of your control. Anyone can use your name in a comment or post and this could show up in any search under that name. There may be other people spreading rumors and misinformation about you for person reasons as well. You should be aware of the existence of this information.

That is why it is important that at least every quarter, or more frequently when you are job hunting, you do your own search on the popular search engines to see what comes up when your name is searched. You should do this for several reasons.

First, your name is not usually unique and others will have your name and it will be exactly your name or maybe have a different middle name but the same middle initial. For example David Donald Jones and David Dennis Jones will both be known as David D. Jones. So if you search under David D. Jones you will get both entries.

If someone with your same name happens to be a rapist or axe murderer and they live near you, that is something you might want to know so you can make others aware of this on a pro-active basis!

If you do find inaccurate information, or embarrassing information on any site, you can always petition to have it removed but most sites will not remove content.

They will cite freedom of speech laws as their reason. If something is blatantly false you may have a shot. But if it's real, then you are pretty much out of luck. Regardless, you should be aware of it so that you can do any damaged control that might be needed to restore your reputation.

Stay Out of Trouble!

The best way to stop trouble is by staying out of its way. That means staying away from situations where your image is likely or possibly to be recorded and put online. If you are stoned or plastered at a concert, figure that someone is likely taking pictures and videos and uploading them to YouTube or some other site. People watch those videos and share them with others and before you know it, you are a viral sensation!

Ask your friends not to share or post pictures or comments about you unless they are positive in nature and something you can be proud of or that will make you look better. And for the record, those half naked pictures of you in Cancun surrounded by empty beer bottles probably are not what you would want an employer to see when they search under your name!

Yes, sometimes we go out and we have fun and we do crazy things. But sometimes those crazy things come back to haunt us and cause us problems down the road. Be very careful what you post and what others may post about you.

Be Aware of Your Surroundings

If you are at places where people are known to record things and take pictures, be on your best behavior. Don't get drunk at a concert or a baseball game. If you want to drink to excess, do it at home. If friends are there, ask them to leave their phones in the car!

There is a large segment of the population that just loves to catch people in negative or embarrassing situations. I'm not sure why that is but they love to record video and share it so everyone gets a laugh at someone else's expense. Don't be that person. Watch what you do whenever you are in public. You never know who is going to wind up seeing what you do minutes after you have done it!

Be Careful What Sites You Post On

Let's be clear on something before we go on. Everyone is entitled to their opinions and everyone is entitled to decide on his or her own what they like, dislike or choose to be for or against. That is the law and that is exactly how things should be.

But an extension of that law is also that we cannot control how others view us when they see us connected to any group, cause, or website. Some sites are main stream while others might be considered controversial to say the least.

You should consider how prospective employers might react if they find out that you support, or are connected to, a particular cause or group. Will this hurt or help your chances of landing a job? Will it make you more or less desirable as a candidate? I am not saying you should tailor who you are and what you do to what others want but you need to understand it could have an effect, both positive and negative, on your chances of landing a job.

What Do Employers Look For?

When it comes to hiring someone, or even evaluating them prior to offering them an interview, companies want to make sure that they getting what they think they are getting. People are not likely to volunteer or share negative information about themselves during an interview or include such information on their resume. Their goal is to make themselves look better not worse.

Since hiring someone new represents a commitment of time and resources by the company, they want to make sure they are getting a high quality individual that is who they portrayed themselves to be on their resume.

They will do a basic search to make sure there are no obvious character flaws or information that portrays a different picture of you. They will search under your name and see what information shows up in the search results.

They might look at Social media to get an idea of who you really are and what the content on your site might be.

They will look to see what sites you post on and what you post about. This is legitimate because people usually post on blogs that talk about their industry and jobs. As we stated before, posting on industry specific blogs is one way of establishing yourself in your area of expertise. In that way discovering those posts is a positive for you. But if you also have postings on blogs talking about satanic rituals, that is not so good.

They might do a credit check to make sure you are responsible with money and that there is no incentive to steal to pay off debts or other things. They will do a criminal records check to make sure you don't use their company car when you had 14 speeding tickets in the last 2 years. That is not so good for you either.

While companies search for these types of things they are not doing it to find out specifics per say but to get an overall idea of the kind of person you really are. A good credit rating, for example, shows that you are responsible and that you manage money well and that you pay your bills on time. It shows you are trustworthy and indicates you are organized as well.

They do all these things to make sure that you are a good fit with their organization and also to protect themselves against hiring someone with a criminal background. Usually these checks are routine but if there is something in your past that has been misrepresented or outright false, you may want to give some thought about how to address it before it is discovered by someone else. It might never be discovered but then again, it is easier to find out these things today than it was a few years ago.

Know Your Goals

It never ceases to amaze me that there are people among us who try to go after what they want in life without really giving much thought as to what they really want! That's like hopping in the car to go on vacation and not knowing whether you are going to Florida or Los Angeles! You might eventually get to where you want to go but you are definitely going to take a lot of wrong turns and you just might run out of time before you get there!

There are different reasons why people do things in their lives and choosing a career or growing one is no different. You might want more money, a greater feeling of purpose or accomplishment, fame or recognition, or in some cases, more power. Any or all of those reasons are not right nor wrong, they are just what drive us to do things in life.

It is important that we understand what we are looking for in our lives and careers. That we really know what we want and why we want it. This will help us make the right decisions so that we can get the best results in the shortest amount of time. It will help us reduce mistakes, save time and give us the best possible chance for success.

Knowing our goals and what is important to us in life also helps us create a lifestyle that gives us the most of what we like and the least of what we dislike. While that sounds extremely basic, it is very true.

For example, let's say that spending time with our family is one of the things in life that you value or treasure the most. If you realize this you would be far less likely to pursue a career change that would take you away from home for extended periods of time. While that change might result in more money, it would also result in having less time to spend with your family. So knowing what you want out of life and your career will help you create the best compromise.

Also understand that there is no one perfect plan or reason to do anything in life. While one direction might be fine for a co-worker or friend, that same direction might be completely wrong for you. That's because we are all different and we all have different likes and dislikes that form our attitudes and approaches to life.

That means that there are very few "wrong" choices when it comes to deciding what you want in life.

I know some people who are very career driven while others place family first and foremost in their lives. I know people who strive for money first and everything else is a distant second while others I know have a low opinion of money and what it brings people. Everything depends on who we are and what we value in life.

That is why it is so important that you understand two basic things at this point. The first one is that everyone is different and that just because something works for one person does not mean it will work for someone else. So don't follow in someone else's footsteps until you have thought long and hard about it first.

The second thing is that YOU are responsible for your life and no one else. Once you leave childhood behind and are capable of understanding certain things in life, YOU become the leader in your life. Parents and friends may guide you and give their input and advice, but it must be YOU that makes the final decision!

Your father might be a world class doctor or lawyer but that doesn't mean you have to be one as well. It might be that you are destined to be a world class painter or teacher or social worker. In many respects what you do is not as important as how well it fits into who you really are.

Yes, there will be pressures from those around you to do what they think is the best for you.

These people mean well and they truly have your best interests at heart but they cannot know what's in your heart. Only you can really know that. Only you know what brings you joy, satisfaction and a sense of accomplishment.

So before we start mapping out our careers and our futures, let's take a few days to look inside to see who we are and what is really important to us. This need not be an involved process and it can be accomplished by doing something as simple as writing down a list of things we like and dislike as well as where we think we want to go in life.

In other words, we want to develop a plan that highlights what we want and how we are going to get there. This plan will never really be done as it will always grow and change as we grow and change. But it will always be there to help us make the right choices and guide us down the right paths in life.

There are only two things that you really need to make up a basic career or life plan.

The first is honesty. You must be totally honest with yourself as you go through this process. Don't convince yourself that something is not important to you when it really is. Don't tell yourself that sacrificing your values is worth a larger pay check because it isn't. Be honest with yourself so that you can make the right choices so you will only have to do things once and not go back and start over again in the future.

Also, don't confuse being honest with being lazy. You might try and convince yourself that you don't really want something because it might mean a lot of hard work to get what you want in life. For example, you might try and convince yourself that you don't want a certain job because it requires a college degree and you don't want to spend 4 years in school. That would be a case of being lazy and not honest. Always be honest with yourself even though it might be painful.

The second thing you need is an open mind. You might travel through some uncharted or difficult places throughout this process where you have to admit certain things about yourself. Maybe you are lazy or maybe you made some stupid choices earlier in life that you now have to recover from. Whatever it is, be open minded about things.

There are very few things we cannot accomplish in life if we know what we want and are willing to put in the time and effort to get there. The key is knowing what we truly want out of life and what is important to us.

A career is just one part of our life. A successful career fits neatly into our lives and makes our life better, richer, more rewarding and happier. The perfect career makes us better as people and does not dominate us. Instead it compliments us. That is why it is so important to understand what we really want out of our career now rather than later.

So take a little while to understand what you want out of your career and your life. Write things down and go back to you list every month or year to make sure you are heading down the right path. Add things you discover along the way that make you happy. Remove things that you no longer find important or meaningful. Remember, as our lives change so do we. It would be a shame if we didn't make the effort to keep up with life.

Embrace Change

One skill that is very useful to have when it comes to growing or establishing a career is the ability to handle and even embrace change. Most people are afraid of change or avoid it and this can lead to missed opportunities and stagnant career growth.

Take it from me when I tell you that if you avoid change or just sit back and wait for something to come to you, it is not likely to happen. In order to take the most from life and your career you need to be able to go out and grab change, embrace it and make the very best out of it.

There is a saying that goes "If you change nothing, nothing changes" and that is very true. In order to get more you have to put yourself in the position to get more. Even the person who wins the lottery had to first go out and buy the damned ticket! You cannot wait for other's to do what you have needed to do all the time!

Another myth is that in order to make a huge change in your life you have to take a huge or drastic action. The fact is, all you need to do to make some very meaningful changes in your life is to take a few small actions or make some small adjustments to help position yourself for the change.

If you want a better job you don't have to quit your current job, move across the country and start from scratch. You can take a few courses, make a few attitude adjustments and position yourself for growth right there in your own community. Will there be some cases where you have to move across the country to grow? Well, yes, depending on your career and marketplace. But that can be your choice and not be something that is always required.

There are two ways you can deal with change. You can experience the change and make adjustments so that you can make the best out of things or you can anticipate change and be ready for it before it arrives. That is called being pro-active and that is the very best way to deal with change. It is far better to anticipate it and be prepared for it than to be caught unaware and have to scramble at the last moment to catch up.

In a previous chapter we talked about knowing what you want and what it will take to get that into your life. That is crucial to being pro-active. By knowing what you want and how to best go about getting it, you can be prepared for opportunity when it arrives.

This is important because if you are not prepared then opportunity can pass you by.

For example, if you have given some thought as to what lies ahead for you in life, you might have uncovered your next idea career path and the job that will help you achieve your goals. With that information in mind, you can take steps now to prepare yourself for later. That might mean making sure you have all the requirements for the job now or allowing yourself time to get those requirements before you need them.

Let's say you are a middle manager and you realize the best opportunity right now would be for you to get a department manager position in either your company or a similar company in your town. So you research the job and find out what the requirements are for the job. You find you need a certain certification or degree and you take steps to get that certification or degree now. You craft the best possible resume tailored to that particular job and you even do some volunteering or get some relevant experience to make yourself appear better to prospective employers.

Now, a year later when that position opens up, you have the qualification all in order, you have your resume in hand that only requires some minor changes to bring itself current and you have some relevant experience in your back pocket.

In other words, you are ready to go when that opportunity presents itself. No waiting, no scrambling, you are all set to take advantage of that opportunity!

Now let's look at what a lot of people do. They have not given their next step much thought. Even if they have, they haven't done anything to prepare themselves for their future opportunity. So the job becomes available and they find out they need a degree or certification they don't have and that will take them 6 months to get if they start right now. They also have no relevant experience and this puts them behind most other applicants. Plus they need a week or two to really get a first class resume put together and submitted.

The result is they are not likely to be considered for the position because they are not desirable candidates. They do not meet the qualifications, they do not have any experience and their resumes look like they were thrown together at the last minute because they were thrown together at the last minute!

Change is all around us. There is almost no career that is the same today as it was a decade ago. Some careers were not even around a decade ago! Technology changes as fast as we change our shoes. What worked for us today is not likely to work as well tomorrow and a few years from now is not likely to work for us at all!

So let's all agree that they best way to deal with change is to be pro-active and prepare ourselves for what lies ahead. The question we should be asking ourselves at this point is not whether I should do something but what I should be doing now to prepare for later.

That is another area where your goals and plan come into view. You will generally find there are things you can do that will help you today and tomorrow while other things will benefit you further on down the line. That means you should be prioritizing the things you do so that you can not only take advantage of what you are doing now but also be prepared for what you will need later.

For example, if you can take a course now that will qualify you for a promotion or a pay raise, then you should take that course now so you can reap the rewards now rather than later. But if you also need to do something to help you get a promotion two years from now you would complete the course now and then work on the other things.

This does not mean that you get to put off things for later just to avoid doing them today. If you have the time now to get something done you should always do that. Being pro-active will prepare you for more now and later.

But if there is something that will give you a benefit NOW, then do those things first and then move on to the other things you will need further on down the line.

To confuse you even more, there will be things you will need to do in order to keep up with changes or hopefully stay ahead of it. A classic example of this is to keep yourself educated on the changes in your own industry or marketplace. This kind of activity is on-going meaning that you never really complete the task. Technology and business are always changing so once you do get current something new is always coming around tomorrow!

But it is important to understand that it is always better to keep yourself current than to allow yourself to fall behind and then have to do a last minute cramming session when you need it. Remember that increasing your knowledge gradually and always being current will help you do a better job today and create a better impression in the eyes of others as well.

I cannot impress on you the importance of embracing change and staying ahead of it whenever possible. Once you get behind it is much more difficult to catch up. Think of a ball rolling downhill. It starts out slowly and it is easy to catch. But the longer you let it roll the faster it gets and the more difficult it becomes to catch. Eventually it becomes impossible to catch and you're done!

Last, but certainly not least, do not for even one minute think you can avoid change. Do not think your career or position is immune to change because it isn't. Everything changes. Computer systems change and so does the software those systems run. Products change, health changes and people change as everything changes around them.

Understanding that you cannot escape change and understanding the value of embracing it will serve you well throughout your life in many other ways other than your career. Don't be the person who gets left behind or the person no one wants to take a chance on. Instead be the person everyone looks towards for help because their skills are the very best.

In other words, be ready and willing to change and adapt.

Your Unique Selling Position

When it comes to getting your first job or any new job or promotion, you have to be able to demonstrate to others that not only can you handle the position but that you are the best choice for that position. It is not good enough to be the best person for the job you have to KNOW you are the best and be able to convince others of that as well!

Put yourself in the position of the person responsible for hiring a new employee. That person has that job because they have been known for being able to choose the best person from a stack of resumes or an inbox full of applications. If you were that person, you would want to choose the very best person for every position because YOUR future depended on it!

Now ask yourself how that person makes their decision. Unless you are applying for a CEO position or something that high up the chain chances are the interviewer is going to rely on your application, resume and your performance at the interview or interviews. They are not going to hire a private investigator or anything like that. They will do a criminal check as a matter of security but that's about it.

So this is more than just who is the best person for the job. What it IS about is who is able to "sell" themselves and convince someone they are the best choice. In fact, and this may comes as a shock to some of you but the best person doesn't always get the job. But the person who best sells themselves usually does get the job!

Another way of looking at this is to think of yourself as a "product" and the consumer as the interviewer. When you buy a product what do you look for? You look at the product description to read about the products features and benefits. You look for product reviews and any other information you can find. But what really brings in the sale are the features, benefits and advertising associated with that product.

So in the case of getting that new job, you are the product, your resume is a list of the features and benefits and your performance at an interview are the advertising content and product reviews.

All of these things point in the same direction. They point to your **Unique Selling Position**.

In advertising or sales, the unique selling position is what makes a particular product special, different and better. It includes features, benefits, price and other factors. To the consumer, if the unique selling position is the best match to their particular needs or requirements, that product is the one they usually choose.

When it comes to your career and your future, you need to understand what your unique selling position is as well. You need to be able to understand what makes you the best fit for any job and what you have to offer that most other people cannot duplicate.

Then you need to be able to use that information to separate yourself from the rest of the applicants. You cannot just have what a job requires you have to be able to show someone why you are the best one for the job. You can't let someone else try and connect the dots. You have to LEAD them through the process. If you allow any doubt to creep in the position could go to someone else even if they are less qualified.

Here are a few things to consider when thinking about what you have to offer any prospective employer or recruiter:

Education

When it comes to education, employers are not just looking at relevant education they are looking for indications that you are capable of learning what you will need to know for the job. A college degree, for example, is not going to teach you the specifics of working for a specific company and on their specific systems.

But what that degree will tell them is that you have demonstrated the ability to learn a wide range of information when required to. The degree is as much a demonstration of knowledge already learned as it is an indication of your ability to learn in the future. It eases doubts in the mind of the interviewer or recruiter.

There are also types of education other than your standard college degrees. There are seminars, apprenticeship programs and education you received during the course of performing similar duties in the past.

Take a few moments to write down the education you have received so far in life. Write down everything you can think of. Write down every seminar, class, lecture, degree or course you have taken. Add to this list anything new you take in the future as well. After all, this can prove to be a great resource when trying to match your education to the requirements of a job. Even though you might not meet the requirements exactly, often times you can substitute other forms of education and still be considered. But this happens only when you make sure these are pointed out.

Skills

While education is great and knowledge is power, all the education in the world is not going to do you much good if you don't know how to use it in the real world. In other words, you need the skills and aptitude to turn what was on paper into something in reality.

There are many skills people value in this world. Mechanical skills may be very important, analytical skills can come in handy and good old common sense is sometimes totally missing in some people as well. Well qualified applicants are people who possess a wide variety of skills.

If someone asked you what skills you are most proud of, could you answer them? I certainly hope so because that question is bound to come up in many forms during any interview. You need to make sure you let people know that not only do you possess the knowledge but that you really know how to USE IT!

Just like we did with our education, write down the skills you posses, especially the ones directly relevant to your current position or where you want to go in life. But even those skills that are not directly relevant should be listed as well. You never know when you can turn one skill into an advantage on a resume or during an interview.

Create a list of the skills you possess and also the skills you think would be an advantage for you to go out and get. Then start acquiring those skills! As you acquire them, add them to your list.

Communication Skills

Speaking of skills, there are no skills more useful in any career or position as communication skills. If you are a great communicator then you will usually go further in life than most other people. Communication skills are among the most sought after skills in the world today. If you posses them, use them. If you don't possess them, GET THEM!

The most common and valuable communication skills are listening, negotiation, conflict resolution, problem solving, and public speaking. If you can master public speaking and listening skills you will find yourself accomplishing more in less time and making fewer mistakes. All of that just makes it easier to bring success closer to you!

Experience

Employers love people with experience. But you can only get experience by getting a job, right? Well, that is not necessarily true. There are many type of experience that will help you get what you want in your career.

You can volunteer your time to get experience in various organizations; you can join an apprenticeship program or take a job training program. You can find a mentor to teach you through one of the mentoring programs that are usually offered in your community.

But the most common experience is the experience you get from your past and current jobs. If you are one of those who do the bare minimum and watch the clock all day you may find yourself a little bit light on the experience part. Smart people take advantage of work to get the training and experience they need on someone else's time and using someone else's money at the same time.

That means volunteering for more projects, learning more things and taking on more responsibility. This not only broadens your background but it also shows initiative as well. People look for people who get involved and do not shirk from work. They look for people with a demonstrated history of doing more than most others and are interested I getting things done!

Experience can be divided into two very basic and broad types. Those two groups are directly relevant and not directly relevant experience. Directly relevant refers to experience that directly pertains to your job or position.

For example, if you are a computer programmer than your experience in programming computers and learning programming languages would be directly relevant. If you are a salesman, then prior experience in sales would be considered relevant. That is because the experience is both these examples are exactly what you are being evaluated for right now.

Experience that is not directly relevant includes things you have done that are outside your normal ob responsibilities. For example, if you are in sales now but you used to be a computer programmer that would be not directly relevant experience. But even this type of experience can be helpful and even critical for you.

Let's say you are selling home appliances but want to get into computer sales. If you used to be a computer programmer that would be an indication that you probably have a better understanding of computers on a deeper level than other applicants. IN this case not directly relevant experience might even be considered directly relevant for this type of position. Regardless anything you can use to increase your perceived value would be smart to include on your resume and also to make other people aware of.

Make a list of all the things you have done. Don't leave anything out because you never know when you can use something to make yourself look a little bit better than the other applicants.

This is especially critical when it comes to resumes because if your resume isn't impressive you may never get to an interview!

Personality

Do you know how others think of you? Are you the happy person or sad individual? Are you bright and cheery or dull and listless? The kind of personality you have can either be an asset or liability for you.

While no one should expect you to change who or what you are, the reality of things are that people who are positive and cheerful generally make a much better impression than those who dwell on the negative and appear withdrawn or shy.

Personalities also help people form a certain impression about you as well. If your particular personality makes people trust you or like you, that should be considered a major asset to you. You should be aware of this and use it to your advantage. Depending on which career you decide on, or which position in your company you are targeting, personality may play an important or marginal role.

Do a personality evaluation to see if there are any parts of your personality that you should work on or change. Ask friends and relatives, even a co-worker or two that you can trust what they think.

Sometimes you might hear things you don't want to hear but this might be the only way you will earn the truth.

Don't get angry just accept the criticism and create something better out of it.

Attitude

Sometimes a great attitude will trump more education and more experience. People with the right attitude are shown to accomplish more in less time and get better results as well! If you have an extremely positive "can do" attitude, then you should be aware of it and make sure others are aware of it as well!

Use your positive attitude to take on more responsibility and show others that you are the one to turn to when something has to get done and get done right. I have seen people with less education and experience get chosen over others for this very reason. If you have the right attitude, put it out there for everyone to see. If you don't have the right attitude then GET IT!

Intangibles

Like we said before, everyone is different and every situation is different as well. Because of this we all have some "intangibles" that help separate us from everyone else. Sometimes these intangibles will carry little weight but sometimes they can be turned into game changers!

Intangibles can be resources that you have access to, accomplishments that carry a certain image or respect with them such as being an Eagle Scout or winning a National Award of some kind, or anything that helps make you more desirable in the eyes of others.

In some cases an intangible might be that you are especially good looking or attractive to others. In some careers this can have a huge value for you. Clothing sales, modeling and being a spokesman are some examples of positions where looks might play a more important role. This is not to say that you flaunt your looks but you should be aware of them and use them whenever you feel it is appropriate.

Think hard about those "little things" that you possess that others might not. Think about the things you do well that might be a benefit to others. Each one of these things can help "tilt the scales" in your favor!

If you really want to do something interesting, give some thought about those things you are not very good at, or perhaps never really tried, that might help you in the future and then get started learning those things or developing those skills.

How can you discover what those things are? The answer might very well be staring you right in the face. Look at the people you respect or admire in your life. They could be friends, relatives, co-workers or anyone else.

Now think about why you feel the way you do about them. What do they do that you appreciate? What makes them appear to be so special?

It just makes sense that if you admire or respect those qualities then others will as well. So take one or two of those things and work on them to develop them and put them to use in your life. Very often it's not the major things that make the difference but some little thing that sticks out in the minds of others that really counts.

Relevance

So far we have mentioned a few of the most common items that help make up your Unique Selling Position. While there are more things to be considered depending on your own situation it is important that we take the time to make ourselves aware of these things.

But just as important is being able to take these special things we have and make them relevant to what we are trying to achieve at that moment. You must not leave it to chance that someone will put the pieces of the puzzle together for you. Most of the time this will not happen by itself. You will have to push the process along.

It is YOUR responsibility to create a personal "sales pitch" that leads other people to the realization that you are the best choice for the job or for that particular situation.

YOU need to show why you are the best choice! YOU need to connect the dots and link your experience and qualities directly to the situation and show that they are relevant.

This is where so many people go wrong. They have the qualifications and they possess the skills. They have little things that make them superb candidates and they think that will "show through" in their resumes, interviews or personal conduct. But the fact is that most of the time it really doesn't. People might appreciate something about you but not really understand what that "something" really is.

That is why one of the most important processes whenever you are trying to get a new job, start or grow a career or better yourself in any way is to understand what you have to offer and then figure out how to make sure people know what you have and how it directly benefits THEM. You need to show them how your particular skills and experience will have a direct impact on your ability to do the job and produce great results.

Here is another tip that most people just don't do. They look at their skills and abilities and they figure out how to use them to their advantage when going after a certain job or promotion. But they stop short of the finish line. They reach the point where they say "All right, that pretty much shows them I'm a good candidate for the job."

Well, sometimes, in fact most of the time, good is just not good enough.

Your approach should be to create a feeling about you that makes the other person forget about everyone else they have talked to or interacted with concerning the job. Your impression should be so strong that there is no question in anyone's mind that they should choose you over anyone else.

We will get into this again in a later chapter but as far as your Unique Selling Position is concerned, right now we need to develop our unique selling position and then understand how we can or should use it to help us get where we want in life.

Connecting the Dots

If you are going to start or grow a career, or move yourself forward in any capacity, you are likely to have to do that in competition with other people who have the same goals and desires. If you are the only one going after a certain job, position or career, one might pause to ask why you really want it in the first place when no one else does!

It is also important to understand that being chosen for a particular job or career is not the result of one particular act or event. It is the sum of many different tasks and events that occur throughout the entire hiring or interview process.

While your end goal should always be to emerge the winner, your intermediate goals should always be doing whatever is required to proceed to the next step in the process. Being able to hit it out of the park with step 3 will not do you any good if you are eliminated during step 2.

So we should be concentrating on getting to the next level while still keeping our eyes on the final goal or prize.

We also need to understand something important and get a little reality check. You will have competition for most things in your career and that competition is likely to be greater than it was for your father or grandfather. That is because every single job, career or opportunity today can be considered a global one and not a local one.

In your mother's or father's time they had to complete against people in their own town or county for the job. In some cases you might include the state as well. But today, when jobs and opportunities are posted on the Internet, you can get applications and resumes from all over the world depending on the job posted. So what might have been limited to maybe 50 applicants but now gather 1,000 applicants from all over.

While that's the bad news, there is good news. The good news is that you are no longer limited to local opportunities either. You can now see opportunities all over the country or the world. Your perfect job might not exist in your state but could be available elsewhere. So even though the competition is higher, the numbers of opportunities are higher as well.

But wait, it gets even better........

By reading this book, you are already ahead of most other applicants. I say that because this book will give you tactics and information that others just won't have! But wait because it gets even better!

A large percentage of the people that apply for jobs or positions don't do the things they need to in order to be successful. Even some of the people who read this book won't do even some of the things they should do to separate them from everyone else! They will see a job posting, slap a generic resume in an envelope or attach it to an e-mail and consider their job done. Believe me when I say that those people should not be considered competition at all!

I want you to be different. I want you to look at the entire process differently. I want you to see what is involved and how you can take simple steps to separate yourself from everyone else that applied. It's not all the difficult and it doesn't take all that much time either. In fact, it can be so easy that you will wonder why other people don't do it. But remember, you should be glad they don't!

A Different View on Career Advancement

Some people believe that you advance your career by printing up a hundred generic resumes at the local copy center and applying for jobs that will earn you more money, prestige or whatever in life you are looking for.

But career advancement is so much more than that. You need to look at career advancement as a process and not a singular act.

Though the process can vary depending on the position you are looking for as well as your own situation, the parts of the process will usually follow these steps:

Positioning

If you are looking to advance your career or move to the next level in your job, there might be things you need to do in order to qualify for the position. At this point you want to determine what those requirements are and make sure you either have them or make plans to get them.

But you should not plan on getting the requirements for any job you should plan on exceeding them! If you come into the process with the minimum qualifications, you might quickly be eliminated if several other people have better qualifications, more education and more experience.

This is the time where you position yourself so that you are in the best possible place for success. It requires looking and planning ahead and being pro-active. IN other words, you need to know where you want to go and what it takes to get there. It requires up front planning and preparation.

You should be aware that if you disregarding this part of the process you might not get any further.

So put in the time and effort now so you will be in the best position to move forward.

Preparation

This is where we prepare ourselves for what lies ahead. This is where we gather information on our skills, talents, and abilities that will help us get the most out of the process. We need to understand what we bring to the table and lay it all out so that we will have a good idea of which jobs we will qualify for when we see them.

This is important because most of us are more qualified than we realize. Without doing this bit of discovery and understanding all we have done so far in life we may falsely exclude ourselves from some really great opportunities!

I am not saying to make up things or convince yourself you are more qualified than you really are. What I am saying is that everyone should know exactly what they can bring to the table and take full advantage of it. Sometimes one little tidbit or experience or education can make all the difference in the word.

Identification

This is where you identify potential opportunities or positions that meet your goals and needs. That means sorting through different opportunities and choosing the ones that best fit what you are looking for.

There are a few ways to go about this part of the process. Naturally you will want to pick the opportunities that you are well qualified for and have a good chance of being successful. After all, going through the process and attending interviews is time consuming and you want to get the most value for your time.

But it is all right to shoot a little higher and apply for a couple of "stretch" positions as well. You might find a great one and get a little lucky and make it through. You do not want to apply just for "stretch" positions though. One or two is fine and the rest should be for legitimate positions that you are qualified for.

Resume

Most people think of their resume as a listing of what they have done and what they know. But it is much more than that. You should not look at your resume as a listing but rather as an advertisement for you. It is your "sell sheet" that has the sole purpose of getting you into the next level.

Unless you are going for a position where you know the people who are hiring, or unless you have a personal connection or recommendation your only way to sell yourself is with your resume.

Though we will be getting into resumes in more detail in a little while, let me just impress one thing on you. I don't care what position or job you are going for.

It might be a CEO position or a mail room position. Regardless of the position do NOT create one generic resume and send it out to every company! That is resume suicide!

Every resume you send to any company should be tailored specifically for that exact job you are applying for. It is all right to have a basic framework stored on your computer from which you work from. But you need to tailor your experience and education to the specific job in order to be successful!

Your thoughts right now should be on creating the resume that will give you the very best chance of getting called in for an interview. Be accurate, be specific and use your resume for the sole purpose of getting in for an interview. If your resume fails to get you the interview you are done so pay attention to this very important step.

Interviews

If you are fortunate to be called in for an interview you are already a winner! That is because whether or not you actually get the job just participating in the interview will give you powerful knowledge you can use on future interviews. The fact is most people fail in their first interview because everything is new and unknown and they get nervous or afraid.

Interviews are where you let your own personality shine through and where you get to tell people just why they should hire you and not anyone else. This is where you have visual contact with your prospective employers and where you can create your most powerful perception ever!

Though we will talk about interviews in depth in a little while, let me just say the interview is where we can compensate for weaker experience and education. The interview is where our attitude and personality takes over and we can impress people in other ways that cannot be placed on paper.

Negotiation / Acceptance

If we make it to this point, then we have proved to ourselves that we did everything pretty well up to this point. We have demonstrated our skills and abilities and have convinced someone to choose us over other people.

At this point it is up to us to determine if this is really in our best interests. Sometimes throughout the process we might discover the position is not what we thought or that it is different than what was described or advertised. We might have found out more than we knew before and have discovered this is not really what we wanted.

Just because someone offers you a position does not mean you have to accept it. And you should feel comfortable knowing what you expect and negotiating for as much of what you want as possible.

In extremely basic term that is the entire process most people go through in their career advancement efforts. The entire process is a series of steps and at every step your focus should be on advancing to the next step.

No matter where you are in the process, your efforts should be focused on making sure you present yourself in the best possible light and doing so in such a way that there is no doubt that you are someone who can do the job and achieve high results.

That means telling a story in your preparation, your resume and your interviews. It means preparing well before you get started and then crafting your "story" and leading people through your story step by step and showing them how and why you are the best choice. It means leaving nothing to the imagination and eliminating confusion and making everything crystal clear.

A long time ago I interviewed for a job that I eventually got. Years later I was having a drink with the person who hired me and he said to me "You know, when I got back to my office after doing all the interviews, you were the only one I remembered. It was really strange."

It was then I knew everything I did, and how I did it, really worked. I had connected all the dots.

And I got the job……..

The 3- Ps

We are going to follow a simple format for our approach to career advancement and growth. It is a three part plan centered around three independent factors. Those 3 factors are Preparation, promotion and Performance. Everything we are going to do will fall in one of these 3 areas. All three areas are important and if you only do one or two of the 3, your results might suffer.

The great news is that anyone, and I mean anyone, can easily master all 3 areas and easily implement them without any specialized knowledge, education or skill sets. If you can read this book and do some basic writing, you are good to go.

As we get started in this book I will give you a short overview on each of these 3 important areas. We will go into more detail as we go on but for now, this short explanation will give you what you need to understand to see what we are going to learn and why all three areas are so important.

Here are the three areas in our career advancement strategy:

Preparation

Sometimes the things we do that have the most benefit are the things we do to prepare ourselves for what lies ahead. That means doing things today that will prepare us and set us up for success tomorrow.

In the case of job hunting or furthering a career preparation might include obtaining the education, certifications or licenses you might need to move your career to the next level. It might mean spending time gathering information on the companies you are interested in working for or spending time today designing and improving your most current resume or updating an older one.

Another example of preparation might be taking a few practice interviews before going out on some real ones. Whatever you think might help you get ready for the next phase of your career would be examples of preparing yourself for the opportunities yet to come.

Promotion

If you want something in life you usually have to go out there and get it. It usually does not come to you!

The only way you can get a better or new job is to put yourself in the best possible position to get it! IN other words, you have to make other people aware that you are interested and qualified for any opportunity that you are aware of.

That means you need to promote yourself, your skills, your talents and everything about yourself that will factor in to you getting a job offer. Self promotion, if done properly, will expose you to the people and organizations that are best able to help you get the job you want and help take your career in the direction you want it to go.

You can do the best preparation and perform at your very best as well but if people don't know about you they might never give you the opportunity to show them who you are and what you have to offer them. That is why self-promotion is so important when it comes to your career.

Performance

You can do your preparation and promote yourself to the best of your ability but all that will be for naught if you cannot perform when you need to. That means taking what is on your resume and demonstrating it to an interviewer or other people.

This is where many people fall short of expectations. People get scared or nervous and they freeze up or lose their nerve.

Fortunately there are easy ways to deal with this and we will share them with you throughout this book. There is nothing to fear and eventually you will come to that understanding all by yourself.

Your ability to perform comes into play during interviews or phone conversations. This is one area where your preparation will help you craft the best answers to even the most difficult questions. This is where knowing what you are going to say before you need to say it will reduce stress and nervousness and allow you to do your best!

So these are the 3 P's that are going to help you get the job and the career you want for yourself. Please understand that these 3 processes work well when used separately as well as together. Preparing for anything is always a smart idea. Promoting yourself in the right way will get you noticed in your industry as well as bring you respect in the marketplace. Last, but certainly not least, your ability to perform at your highest level will bring you the respect you need to convince people you are qualified and ready for bigger and better things.

But it is when we combine all 3 of these steps that they really come to work for you in a powerful way to bring you more success than you ever thought possible. It is a case where individual things come together to act even more powerful than they were individually.

It should also be mentioned that all three of these steps are never really finished. They continue to change and evolve as you change and evolve. There is always something new to learn about or prepare for and there will always be opportunities to promote yourself as well.

Never be satisfied to be where you are. Always look for ways to be better at something than anyone else. Always look for ways to make yourself more visible in your job, your community and your industry. And always practice your craft and strive to be the very best you can be in whatever you do. Never be satisfied by just being good enough. Always strive to be the best.

If you commit to all three parts of the process you WILL be successful. There is no doubt about that. But success means different things to different people. So take your time, watch the 3 P's and make a commitment to yourself to use all three parts and not just one or two.

As I said, if you do all three, you will be successful!

Your Resume

Even though this is not a book on resumes or resume preparation, any book on career advancement or growth would not be complete without a discussion on the importance of having a great resume.

Resumes are sometimes the only way you can sell yourself to other people when it comes to job hunting or promotion. In fact, unless you are looking within your own company or have a personal connection or introduction, your resume is how you will penetrate into other companies or organizations.

Some people think your resume is the way you convince someone that you are the right candidate for the job. I guess on some level this might be true but the fact is the most important function of a resume is to get you an interview.

If your resume looks great but doesn't lead you into an interview, then your resume has not served its purpose.

So in this chapter we will give you a few pointers on how to go about creating and designing your resume. We're not going to go into formatting or structure but instead the functionality of how your resume should read when being looked at by others.

With this in mind, here are a few things you should consider when crafting your resume:

Your Sales Letter

As you craft your resume, keep in mind that your resume is in fact your personal sales letter. It is being used as an advertisement to sell you, the job applicant. If you look at your resume in this manner you will understand that everything you put in your resume should there for a reason.

Your resume should include those items that make you look the best and make you as impressive as you possibly can be. Do not lie but do not be modest either. If you have an outstanding achievement that makes you look good for a particular opportunity or position, find a way to include that and make it relevant.

Your resume is your first opportunity to separate you from the other hundreds of applicants. So it has to stand out.

It has to deliver memorable content that makes the reader want to take your resume out of the pile and save it for further reading. It should not just state what you have done or where you went to school. It should market and promote YOU!

Research First

As with promoting any product, you have to know your market first. In the case of job hunting or resumes you need to understand the basics about the company you are applying to and what they are looking for. Once you know this you can tailor your resume accordingly.

Understand the products or services the company produces and how your experience and education could be relevant to that particular company. Make sure that comes across in the content and wording that you place in your resume.

Your resume should impart the feeling that you are a good fit to the company and that your experience and background are relevant and impressive. Target every bullet point in the ad or job posting and make sure you address each and every one if you have anything relevant that pertains to each job responsibility.

You may also look for a specific person or department to send your resume to even if it is different than what is stated in the ad.

Remember the more people who see your resume the better off you will be. Plus, keep in mind that the person listed in the job posting is going to see hundreds, perhaps thousands, of other resumes. If you can send it to someone else, they might actually read it through and submit it with a recommendation. It might not make a difference but then again it just might.

All Resumes Are Not Created Equal

Of all the things that someone could do to eliminate them from most of the opportunities out there today, creating one resume and sending it to every available job opening is the most common. It is a grievous mistake and one that is very close to stupidity and laziness.

When I was younger and looking for a job it was difficult to have more than one resume. You had to type each one separately if it was different than another one and then mail it out. Today with computers and word processors, it is downright easy.

Today you can have any number of different resumes in different styles and each with different content. You could have one for each type of position you are interested I and each of those could be individually tailored for each specific opportunity you are applying for. So, let's just agree that having just one resume for everything is just plain stupid and lazy. Don't be one that chooses that route in life.

Instead send out resumes that are carefully crafted and worded to take advantage of that particular opportunity or job positing. You can create a standard framework if you want but do in and modify it to be specifically relevant to one specific application.

Change the order in which things appear to match the job requirements or other bullet points in the posting. Include specifically targeted information that makes you appear to be the perfect "fit" for that job or opportunity. Use your resume to connect the dots between what is listed in the application and your particular background.

Every word, every bit of content, and the order of that content should be chosen to enhance your suitability for that position. If something isn't relevant, eliminate it. If something should be in there and it isn't add it. Spend the time to create the most targeted and complimentary resume you possibly can.

Remember, this is the one document you can use to get invited in for a personal interview. Take full advantage of that and create your most perfect "sales letter".

Short, Sweet and to the Point

Remember when we said that today job postings often gather hundreds or thousands of resumes?

Add to that resumes for other positions or those just seeking work from those looking to enter the job market for the first time and the task of reading and processing all of those resumes can get overwhelming and downright tedious.

Today it is even rumored that some companies scan the resumes using machines that look for certain words or phrases and they "spit out" resumes for second looks. Either way, people reading or processing resumes do not want to read through a 14 page novel about your experience and education and hobbies. They want it short, concise and to the point.

A one page resume is best but it is hard to get all your education, experience and contact information onto one page while still using a font size that can be read without magnifying glasses! So your particular resume might be two pages but it should definitely not be more than two.

Start out listing everything you feel should be in your resume and using the font sizes you feel are optimal. Then see how long your resume is at that point. If it is two pages or less you are in pretty good shape. But if it is 3 or 4 pages long, you will need to shorten it a bit.

Since you want to make your resume the most powerful and impressive as possible, you don't necessarily want to remove anything from it unless you really have to.

You can look to see if there are items that can be combined into one longer item that hits both topics. That can save space. For example if you have two lines like "I was responsible for a sales territory handling $5,000,000" followed by "I was responsible for the hiring & management of sales associates" you might combine both of them into something like "I was responsible for a sales territory handling $5,000,000 in annual sales as well as the hiring and management of all sales associates. This might not sound like a major change but it would remove one line and even that could get you from 3 pages down to 2 without removing any valuable content.

Another possibility might be to reduce font size. Be careful with that and don't go below 10pt because anything smaller might be too hard to read and your resume might be tossed aside because of that.

Keep it Relevant

Whatever content you do place in your resume, make sure it is listed in such a way that it is relevant to the position you are applying for. You should connect the dots and lead the reader through everything and explaining to them bit by bit leaving nothing to chance.

If something does not apply to what you are applying for, and if it does little or nothing to enhance your suitability for the position, then get rid of it. You will only have one chance to get your resume read.

Usually people will scan through a resume first to see if something catches their eye. If that doesn't happen your resume goes into the trash pile. If the reader gets bored, the resume goes into the trash pile.

Your goal should be to capture the interest of the reader and make them want to read more. You want them to want to learn more about you and your background. Do you know how they learn more about you? In the interview! So if your resume leads someone to invite you in for an interview, it has done its job!

Words of Success

The words you use in your resume have a direct reflection on who you are. If the words you use and grammar make you appear like you an idiot with a 4th grade education you are not going to get very far!

Make sure the words you use are the right ones for the application and that they "flow" correctly. Your resume should be easy to read without long and overly complicated words. It should read like educated people usually use in normal conversation. You should not appear to be an over educated snob who likes to use a 14 syllable word when a 2 syllable word will do just fine.

Even more important, everything should be spelled correctly. Do NOT rely on spell check to catch errors.

Red over the entire resume and make sure the right words are used and that everything is spelled correctly and laid out properly. Misspelled words and a sloppy layout will reflect poorly on you.

One trick many people do when proof reading their resume, or any document for that matter, is to read it backwards. This will allow you to read each word more carefully to check for spelling mistakes. Reading it normally might tend to mask over mistakes because your eyes just flow past them.

Standing Out from the Rest of the Pile

Sometimes it's the little things that make a big difference. One little thing you can do is make your resume stand out from the rest of them on the pile. Use a different shade of paper than white. Use a cream color or light tan so that it is easier to find when needed.

This is more of a psychological issue than anything else. The human eye is drawn to things that are somehow different. So that might draw a person's eye to your resume because it looks different than the rest.

Keep in mind that this is only effective in getting eyes on your resume. It will not make the content look or read better. You still have to have quality content that is relevant to what you are applying for.

Be careful not to use weird paper sizes.

Larger paper might not fit in the folder they keep resumes in and smaller paper will not only hold less content but the smaller size might give the perception of being less impressive or valuable.

The Early Bird Gets Their Resume Read!

In case you haven't realized this yet, one of the continuing themes in this publication is keeping up to date on everything and having every bit of information and content at your disposal so it's there when you need it.

This is especially important when it comes to sending in resumes because the earlier you get your resume in the better the chances of it being read. Think about that for a minute. If you have everything all reading to go except for some minor tweaking, you can have your resume ready and submitted the same day you see the job posting. Other people will have to take the time to gather information, draft their resume and the overall result is likely to be inferior to those who were ready and set to go.

It stands to reason that if your resume comes in ahead of the rush then the people tasked with reading and evaluating resumes will have fewer to look at when yours arrives. That means that theoretically they will be able to spend more time on each resume. Of course, it is possible that those resumes that come in early will just sit there for a while until there is a whole stack.

But you never know and it makes sense to get in fast and avoid the rush when every other resumes comes flying in!

Cover Letters

As most people are aware, cover letters usually accompany resumes when you apply for a job or opportunity. Even when you submit a resume via e-mail your cover letter content can be in the body of the e-mail with the resume as an attachment unless you use some kind of automated submission software. In that case it might only be a resume that is submitted.

But a cover letter is important because that is another space where you can place targeted information designed to show and convince people that you are the best candidate. Though your cover letter cannot be the great American novel as far as length is concerned, you can let your personality shine through and create a more personal and positive connection.

In your cover letter, which should be no more than one page, follow the same approach as you should have done with your resume. Keep it short and keep it relevant. Use the space to tie your own experience to those things the company is looking for. Make sure you hit as many points as you can while still making the letter flow nicely and keeping it the proper length.

Your cover letter should be an introduction to your resume. Hopefully it causes the reader to want to learn more about you and provide them with a good reason to give your resume more than a cursory glance. Remember that the longer someone stays reading your resume the greater impression they will get of you and what you bring to the table.

The Growing Resume

A great resume is never really finished either. Once you spend the time and effort into crafting the best possible resume, you should also take the time and effort to constantly update it as your experience and accomplishments grow.

Over time more recent history will replace older entries on your resume as well. When you are 40 years old no one really cares where you worked in the summer when you were in High School so those entries will go away and be replaced by more recent, and hopefully more impressive, entries.

This process should continue until you are close to retirement. Your resume should always grow with you. No one knows when you will need your resume in a hurry. Opportunities don't give much notice and companies go out of business without notice as well. Do yourself a favor and always keep a resume current. You'll never know when you will need it I a hurry!

Summary

Always think of your resume and cover letters as your first attempt to sell yourself to a prospective company or organization. It should be designed to create interest and curiosity about you so the person recommends that you be brought in for an interview. That is the primary goal at this point.

Do not skimp on your resume. Writing resumes does require a certain amount of writing skills. If you do not feel comfortable writing your own resume, ask a friend or family member to help you. Another option might be to hire a professional to create a resume for you.

Generally speaking, the more important or higher paying the job the more important your resume is going to be. But even someone entering the job market for the first time needs to have a professional looking resume. Your resume is a direct reflection on you and it should be as flawless and perfect as it can be.

Though I have skirted this issue so far it is time to state what should be obvious. Your resume should be designed to make you look as good as you can possibly be while remaining factual. You should not lie or state falsehoods in your resume. Certain things like college degrees and previous work experience are easy to check on.

If it is found that you have lied about anything on your resume, no matter how small, you will have kissed any chances of getting that job goodbye. You will likely ruin your chances with that company in the future as well.

The more time and effort you put into building your resume the more successful you will be in getting the job and career you want in life. Don't think even for a single moment that your resume isn't one of the most important parts of advancing your career. It is the document that is most responsible for getting your face in front of the people who need to see it!

Interviews

Everyone who has ever been hired for a job has had an interview. People just don't hire other people without talking to them first. Interviews can take many forms but they all have one purpose. That is for the person or people doing the hiring to get an in person look and impression of a prospective candidate. After all, you cannot "see" someone in a resume!

Up until this point, there has been little or no personal interaction in the job hunting or career advancement process. That is why so many people get nervous, even frightened, when it comes to going to an interview. That nervousness or fear keeps them from doing their best and creating the best impression they possibly can.

As with resumes, entire books have been written on how to handle different types of interviews. If you have never experienced an interview, it might be a good idea to read one of those books to take away some of the fear of the unknown.

But if you have had an interview or two, you should realize now that there is little to fear during an interview.

Interviewers are not looking to be confrontational or hard on people they interview. They are primarily interested in finding the best candidate for the position that is open. They are not interested in scaring good people away. If you present yourself properly you will be treated with dignity and respect throughout the process. If you do get a real hard-nosed and obnoxious interviewer you should think twice about working for that company anyway!

In an interview you have just one objective. That is to convince the people sitting across from you that you are the very best person for the job. You are not there to become friends or make small talk (unless that helps you in bringing your personality across). You are there to promote yourself and land a job offer. In simple terms, you want to make a great impression.

With that in mind, here are some things to consider before your next interview. They will help you get in the proper frame of mind and allow you to relax and do your best as well.

Be Prepared

So many people walk into an interview without doing any preparation whatsoever.

They feel that their resume has opened the doors so all they have to do right now is walk in. You should thank those people because they have helped you weed out some of the applicants!

You should prepare for every interview you go on. Learn about the company and what they do. If they are known for something special, you should know that as well. Understanding what the company is all about will help you tailor your answers accordingly and make you appear smarter than you might actually be!

Try and anticipate some of the questions you will be asked and figure out how to best answer them. Research this online and be acquainted with some common questions. Believe me when I tell you the interviewer probably researched their questions as well! The better your answers are the better impression you will make!

Know Your Strengths & Minimize Weaknesses

Everyone has weaknesses. If you think you don't have any weaknesses then you are not being honest with yourself. Your focus now should be on realizing what those weaknesses are and figuring out how to minimize them for the interview. That means either turning those weaknesses into strengths by changing something about you or figuring out how to frame your answers to minimize those weaknesses.

For example, if you lack specific education that the company is looking for and you are asked about it, you might reply "Well, I do not have that particular education background but I have 13 years experience actually performing those tasks in the field. I feel that is even more valuable than attending classes or lectures. Unlike someone who has read about how to do something, I have actually done it!"

Every answer should point to strength and something positive. Even minimizing a weakness will make you look better in the eyes of the interviewer. Be careful, however, of appearing over confident or pompous. No one really likes to see that in other people.

Practice Makes Perfect

Nothing beats experience to reduce fear and anxiety. Practicing answering questions will help you with your delivery and confidence. Practice with a family member or friend and hone your responses until they flow naturally and are exactly the way you want them.

Even better, try going on a couple of interviews for positions you don't even feel you are qualified for or that have a limited downside for you. This way you can experience an interview setting and see what it's like without really risking anything other than your time.

There are some schools that teach courses in interviews as well and part of those classes include mock interviews to teach you how to handle them. If you graduated college check with your school to see if they offer this service to their graduates. Most of them offer them and this can help you a lot. Otherwise, check out local business schools or adult education. Local or state employment offices usually offer these classes as well.

Be on Time

If your interview is scheduled for a specific time, and most of them will be, then plan on arriving 15-30 minutes early depending on how far you have to travel. It is better to sit in the parking lot reading a book or going for a cup of coffee instead of risking being late.

Punctuality is critical when it comes to attending your interview. It shows responsibility and it shows you understand the importance of being respectful to others. It is kind of OK for them to keep you waiting but not the other way around. Remember, it is YOU that are trying to impress them and land the job.

Granted there will be times when mass transit will have problems or the roads will be clogged or something else might happen. That is why you should always allow yourself plenty of extra time to get where you need to be.

But if for some reason you cannot avoid being late, make sure you have a cell phone and the number to call to inform them that you will be late. Most people understand these things and will appreciate the advance notice.

Look the Part

First impressions are very important. It is estimated that someone makes an impression about someone they see for the first time in about 3-5 seconds. Think about what they notice first. They notice what you look like even before they hear your voice. They notice your attire and your grooming. They see your tattoos and the 47 facial piercing you have as well!

I mention that sort of tongue in cheek because you have a decision to make as you prepare for the interview. You need to understand the importance of looking appropriately for the position you are interviewing for. Usual interview attire is a suit and tie. If that particular type of dress is against your principles or if you don't want to remove the 47 piercings you have all over your face then be prepared not to be hired for that financial advisor position!

If you have a lot of tattoos on your arm, wear a long sleeve shirt. If you have a blue Mohawk, consider changing your hairstyle to one that is more universally acceptable. It might not be right and it might not be fair but appearance has a lot to d with the impression you make on other people.

In addition, the clothes you wear should be neat and clean and you should be well groomed. You should have showered and there should be no dirt under your fingernail. Your hair should be neat and trimmed as well. The reason for this is that your appearance is a direct reflection on your personal habits. Someone who is neat and well groomed is usually viewed to be more responsible and organized than someone who shows up disheveled and dirty.

Don't Worry, Be Happy! Be Personable

While the interview is a business type experience, you should not be all serious and solemn. Answer the questions in a light and personable manner and let your personality show through. The interviewer wants to see the human being behind the applicant.

That means greeting the person or people with a warm smile and exchanging of a few pleasantries. Let your pleasing personality show through and demonstrate that you are the kind of person that others like to work with and interact with.

Someone who walks in all serious and acts like the world is coming to an end is not the person others usually warm up to. Neither should you be the dry and all business personality either. Let try and be pleasant and approachable throughout the process.

This does not mean you should tell jokes or become so relaxed and comfortable that you use in appropriate language or behavior. Sometimes interviewers will try and get you to exhibit that kind of behavior by using that sort of language to see if you will. Keep thi8ngs light and pleasant but maintain a professional and appropriate attitude and demeanor throughout the interview.

Be Confident but Not Cocky

Answer all questions with confidence and conviction without appearing to be cocky or appearing to have a superior attitude. People can be confident without being obnoxious and sometimes there can be a fine line between the two.

Try and not hesitate in answering or appear to be caught off guard or unsure of your answer. This is where preparation can come in really handy. If you have been exposed to the tough questions before and practiced you answers, responding during the interview will be easy. You should, though, think before you answer so that your answer is what you really want to say and not something that just popped into your head.

Take difficult questions that might highlight a weakness and try and turn them around to showcase a particular strength that might mask the weakness from your answer.

Remember everything you say should be designed to make you look better and more qualified in the eyes of the interviewer.

Connect the Dots

Hopefully you have done your "homework" and know how your education and experience can be directly relevant and applicable to the position you are being interviewed for. But don't assume the interviewer can put everything together like you did. You need to "connect the dots" for them.

If they ask you a question about your education and experience, go through each one telling them what you have done and exactly how that can be applied to the current job you are interviewing for. For example, you might answer a question like this: "Yes, my experience in my last job handling quality inspections will be useful because we used the same XQZ4000 software platform that your company uses. This will enable me to be productive from day one since I already know the system inside out."

Think of each answer as a means to take what they are looking for and showing them step by step how what you have will match their needs. This was you leave nothing to chance and stand a great chance of opening their eyes that you are even more qualified than they originally thought.

Any time you can make someone think you are even better or more valuable than they thought when you walked in that makes a greater impression on them than if you are exactly what they thought and nothing more. Always remember you are there to impress them and sell yourself. Never miss an opportunity to do either!

Be Positive

Interviewers like to see people with a positive outlook on life and work. They want to see people who will look for ways to get things done not reasons to stop and give up. In other words, they like people who just seem to get things done.

Frame your answers so that you can deliver them in a positive manner using positive words. Give examples where something negative happened and you turned it into a positive by solving something others could not. Interviewers love that kind of stuff!

Be positive about your currently life as well as things that happened in the past. Refer to set backs as learning experiences and showcase the positive aspects of life. In other words, be uplifting instead of downcast.

Be Excited!
When you enter the interview, turn on your excited mood.

Act excited about the interview and the position you are interviewing for. Act excited about how what you have done is so relevant that you just know you are the one for the job.

Put life into your answers by citing examples and giving details all the time with a smile on your face. Try and really getting into the answers and the interview and really become excited by it. The interviewer will see you have a passion about what you are doing and this could be a game changer in the way they look at you as an applicant.

Be Relevant

This is important so we will repeat this once more. Every answer to every question should be relevant to the job and company you are interviewing with. Make every reference to the company that you can. Show them you took the time to research the company and how what you do and how you do it will benefit them.

This shows initiative and the importance that you attached to the interview. It also helps to further connect the dots as to how your experience and skills can be relevant to the position. Done correctly, this can make a huge difference in the perception you create with the interviewers.

Be a Problem Solve

Basically, every job or career exists for a reason.

That reason is to perform a function which solves a problem. After all everything needs to be done and we hire people to do those tasks. Those tasks solve problems and the result is that something gets done and gets done correctly.

So if you embrace that your function in any job is to be a problem solver, this will help you to further target your answers to gain the most impact. If you can create the impression in the interviewers mind that you are a pr0oblem solver and not a problem creator, you instantly become more desirable!

Think about it another way. If you were a manager or business owner, would you want to hire people who knew how to solve problems or would you want people who looked to others to solve them for them? You would want people who solved problems!

As a manager or owner, every problem solved by someone else is one less thing you will have to deal with. That makes your job easier and gives you more time to dedicate to what you need to do to solve your own problems! So if you see someone who is going to make your life easier, wouldn't you want to hire them?

Of course you would!

Ask Intelligent Questions

In every interview, there will come a time when you are asked if you have any particular questions.

Most applicants will use this opportunity to ask about money or benefits or some other compensation issue. That is a mistake. Those topics are best left for the next interview or when the job offer is made.

For now, use this opportunity to ask questions that are designed to bring out your best points and showcase them. If your strong suit is sales and you have won awards, then ask sales related questions that will allow the subject of your awards to be introduced into the conversation. If there is something you just know will make you look better, ask a question that will allow that to become known.

This is an opportunity for you to guide the conversation instead of the other way around. Never pass on any opportunity to make yourself look better and more desirable in the eyes of the interviewer.

Focus on the Company

Even though the focus on the interview is you and what you bring to the table, keep the conversation focused on what you can do for the company not what the company can do for you. There will be ample time for that later.

Instead, focus your answers, questions and comments on the things you can do to make things better, easier and less expensive for the company. Make sure that they understand that helping the company is one of your focal points and that you are not just concerned about yourself.

Both you and the interviewer know you are curious about benefits and salary and those things but they will appreciate that you have decided other things are more important at this point in time.

Be Thankful

Always thank the interviewer for the opportunity to interview with them. Even if the interview went poorly and you are not a good fit for the position, it is still important to make a good impression. There are always other opportunities down the road and you want to be considered for those as well, right?

Thank them for the interview, shake their hands and wish them well. Then, when you get home, draft a short letter thanking them again for the opportunity. If there is something you forgot to mention in the interview that you feel has value you can try to work that into the thank you letter as well. But the main focus of the letter should be on saying thank you.

This shows class and respect and is just the right thing to do. Your letter might not even make it to the interviewer but on the off change it doesn't it is worth writing it and sending it out. Do not wait too long to send the letter. You want the person to get it while they still remember which applicant you are.

Follow-Up

It is always a great idea to keep you name and impression in the mind of the interviewer. You can accomplish this by sending a follow-up letter or e-mail a week or so later asking if there are any other questions that they might have that you could answer for them. Tell them how excited you are about the opportunity and how you think you could do a great job for them.

Send one follow-up letter and see what happens. Do not keep sending them. There is a fine line between follow-up and being a stalker! Too many letters might also make you appear desperate. That could hurt you if the job is offered to you. They might feel you are so desperate that they can offer you a lower salary and that you would take it.

Learn From Your Interviews

After your interview, while things are fresh in your mind, do an assessment of how things went and how you thought your performance was. Ask yourself what you did well and what you faltered on. This is important because everyone goes on interviews where they don't get the job. If you can dissect what transpired and learn from it, your performance next time will be that much better.

Don't think that the interview was a failure if you don't get the job. Think of it as a learning opportunity where you can use it to do even better next time. If you learn just one thing that helps you next time, the interview was not a failure!

You Have a Choice

There is one concept that many job seekers or career builders never seem to either think about or comprehend. That is that they are the ones who have to match or conform to what the employer wants and not vice-versa. The employer has an idea or picture of what their ideal candidate should be and if you match that idea or picture you have a great chance of getting the job. If you don't match the picture, well, better luck next time.

I mention this because today people seem to believe that people have to accept them for who and what they are, what they look like and how they act. In life that might be true but when it comes to getting a job, or even keeping an existing one, it's just not true at all.

As we mentioned, you need to decide if you want to do whatever it takes to match that "picture" of what the ideal candidate is supposed to look like in the eyes of the interviewer or employer.

No one is forcing you and it is totally your decision but you cannot expect or demand that someone hire you if you are not what they are looking for.

Let's get something else straight right off the bat as well. For those of you who are screaming prejudice or profiling or anything like that, THAT is NOT what we are referring to. It is not right or acceptable to not hire someone because of their skin color or their gender. That is wrong and against the law.

But if you have bright blue hair, facial piercings and tattoos all over your body that interview for that financial planner is not likely to result in a job. It might be your right to look any way that you want to but that doesn't mean others have to hire you if that look does not fit their image or profile.

There are many "excuses" people might give for not hiring you. They are not likely to say it is your appearance or anything else. They will simply say there were other more qualified people or use some other excuse and you might never be the wiser. But the end result is that you didn't get the job.

Now no one is saying that you can't look, dress or act the way you want to. After all, it's your life. But you need to understand that when we make choices or decisions in life there are consequences. The things we do will either bring us closer to what we really want or take us further away.

So we need to be aware that what we do will either make it easier or more difficult to get the jobs we want.

Some people might say it is wrong for society to make them conform to their idea of what acceptable is. They might even have a valid point. After all, we should not have to conform to someone else's vision of what we should do in life.

But when we make the decision to be different or move away from the mainstream culture that is likely to cause us problems in other areas of life. So you have a decision to make. You can follow your values and moral code or you can change in order to get the job and career you want. You might also consider continuing until you find a company that will hire you but that might take a while.

As for changing the views of society, be aware that most of the meaningful change that occurs in life comes from within. So you might consider changing a little to get the job and then attempt to push the envelope a bit once they get to know you. I'm not saying that will work for you but it is another option.

Be a Problem Solver

No matter what industry you work in, or what position you hold, what you do and how you do it either solves problems or creates problems. It just makes sense that you should try to be one of the people who solves the problems instead of causing them!

People who solve problems are usually in higher demand, have higher salaries, increased upward mobility and higher job security. That is because they are far more valuable to their company.

With that in mind, may we suggest that you change your attitude when it comes to problems and setbacks? Can we convince you it is far better for career growth to become the person known for getting things done and not the person who lets every negative thing or set-back get to them and make them quit?

We need to look at problems and setbacks differently. We need to look at them as a challenge and look for ways to overcome them and stop them dead in their tracks.

We need to solve problems so they never happen again in the future. If we can do that we will become infinitely more valuable to our co-workers and our employers.

Employers want to hire problem solvers because they accomplish more in less time, are far more productive and they have the ability to make the work environment around them better and more productive as well. This translates into increased profits and that is always one thing businesses and employers all look for!

If you are currently employed, get more involved in improving the things around you. When a problem arises, do not hide in the background, Instead, be one of the first people to help resolve it. Learn more about things and help make them better. Never be satisfied with how things are if you can make them better! Develop a pro-active attitude towards problems and solutions. Become the "go to guy" people approach for help and to solve problems. In other words, become a resource.

When it comes to management, they love people who take the initiative and solve problems. They like them because the problems they solve do not have to be solved by them and that makes their jobs easier. It allows them to get more done or it lessens their workload.

Think about how you would look at someone if you were a boss or manager.

If you saw someone who could make your job better and easier, wouldn't you want to hire them? That is looking at things from a selfish point of view but it is accurate none the less.

Every time you take a problem and solve it, make note of it. These situations can be used in interviews to help you create the impression that you are a positive force that takes control and helps make things better.

Make Others Look Good

Most people are very good at making themselves look good. They understand the benefits of self-promotion and take every opportunity to use it to their advantage. But sometimes self-promotion is done to the point where so much focus is placed on the individual that none is left for other people. Some people even take this to such an extreme that they take credit for work actually done by others and that can be very dangerous.

The fact is, if you can make others look good through the work that you do, this can come back to benefit you greatly. This can be especially true if you are looking to advance within the company you currently work for.

When someone works well with others and improves the quality of work for the whole group they are usually referred to as being "team players". Team players are people who like to work together to achieve a common goal.

They are more concerned with team performance than they are individual performance and goals.

Being a team player is a very desirable attribute when it comes to hiring people. Very little is accomplished by just one person. Most objectives require the efforts and input of several people and when people work well together more is accomplished in less time. That means projects get completed faster, better and usually for less money.

Being known as a team player also demonstrates that you possess other valuable skills such as communication skills, self confidence and the ability to place the good of the group above your own good. All of those skills and abilities are viewed very highly by interviewers and Human Resources personnel.

During interviews people candidates who use examples where they helped a group succeed and also viewed highly. It is a great way of showcasing individual skills and abilities without appearing cocky or self absorbed. It is also appreciated that the candidate is not just talking about him or herself but the importance of working with others towards a common goal.

Another benefit is that working well with others and making others look good in the process creates a better and far less stressful working environment for everyone.

It is somewhat rare today to find someone who is not just concerned with their own personal gain.

Always remember that the work environment is a cooperative environment where everyone works together to achieve a common goal. It makes no difference what that goal is or your role in achieving it. What matters is that you demonstrate an interest in advancing not only your own career but the careers of others as well. People who do this are natural leaders and leaders are in high demand these days.

Become a Resource

If you want to find a great way to separate yourself from the rest of the pack, then make the effort to become a resource for certain things at work or in life. Become the person people go to first when they have a problem or a question. People who are known as resources are among the most highly noticed and regarded people in any company.

The best part of becoming a resource is that it not only makes you life and job easier but it makes you more valuable at the same time. So not only does your job get easier, you become better!

The other great thing is that you will find as you go through life that a great percentage of people are content with being good at what they do but nothing more. They want to do their job and nothing more. Those are the people that tend to stay right where they are while others, hopefully like you, are moving up in the company or getting better jobs elsewhere.

So how do you become a resource? Well there are several ways.

The first way is by learning more about something. Knowledge is power and if you know more than anyone else about something, people will come to you for answers. That means people see the value in consulting with you before making a decision or taking action. You can bet that if co-workers feel this way so do those above you!

The second way is by putting yourself out there are getting more involved. People who are involved learn more and develop knowledge you just can't get anywhere else. Personal experience is something that grows over time. So of this knowledge is so specialized that you can make yourself invaluable to others and your company in the process!

Another way you can become a resource is to establish relationships with others with expertise in a particular area or subject. This way you don't have to know everything personally. You just can be the one who knows where to go to get whatever is needed!

One of the benefits of becoming a resource is that you get higher visibility from those above you. As you solve problem after problem and as you help others this will be noticed by upper management and others I the company.

You will also probably be asked to take on more responsibilities or help out in other ways. Thought this might increase your workload, the extra visibility will help you in many other ways. Then, whenever a position opens up that you are interested in, you will have a history and reputation as someone who does a good job and helps others.

Let's also not forget that the more you do and the more you accomplish the more valuable your experience will appear at interviews. In addition, the more examples you can give to show your expertise, the more formidable candidate you will become.

All things considered, it just makes sense to take control of your current job, learn all you can about what you are doing and how it should be done and then use that knowledge to create the best possible impression you can.

All of this leads to increased value, a more positive impression in the eyes of others and increased job security. Companies want to keep their valued employees around. If you are known as a resource, your company will go to great lengths to keep you compared to others with less perceived value.

Become Pro-Active

Are you one of those people who put off things until the last minute? Are you someone who waits until they need something before they go out and do it? Are you the person who waits for something to happen before taking action? If any of these apply to you, then you should re-evaluate the way you do things. Because not only is it effecting your life, it is effecting your career as well.

Most of us do things when we have to. We wait until something happens before we take action even though we are aware that eventually something will need to be done. We also tend to put off things that don't have to be done right now because there is no real urgency. While sometimes that might be understandable, there are significant problems and dangers associated with that type of approach.

Two of the most common problems associated with this type of behavior are lack of notice and our inability to see the future. Either of these problems can cause major problems and stress for those who do not take action when they should.

Lack of Notice

Lack of notice is a major problem because not everything in life is scripted and rarely does everything that is scripted go according to plan. Life is full of things that pop up when you least expect it. You will either be prepared or you will be caught unaware. As far as career growth is concerned, being caught unaware is the same as being caught unprepared.

Opportunities can pop-up at any time. People move jobs unexpectantly, they retire earlier than you thought they would and unfortunately, some people will pass away leaving an urgent need to fill a position. When this happens, people who are prepared will be able to take advantage of those opportunities while the rest of us will miss out. Unfortunately, some opportunities come along only once or twice in life and if we miss them, we might never see it again.

Think about your dream job. What would you have to do if you wanted to get that job? Would you need more education, a particular type of experience or some kind of license or certification? Would your resume support that position as it stands now or would it need to be updated?

Those are just a few of the questions you should be asking yourself. The answers will let you know what you need to do. Now the questions should be "When am I going to start?" This is where being pro-active comes into play.

Pro-active means doing things before they need to be done or before they are needed at all. People who are pro-active do not plan on meeting a deadline; they plan on getting the task done now rather than later even if it is due in 3 weeks. Being pro-active also means taking care of something you know needs to be done eventually even if there is no urgency to get it done right now.

Those who get things done now get to do those things on their schedule and usually at their own pace without outside pressures or distractions. In other words, they have the flexibility to tailor their own day to get the most out of it. Those who wait until the last minute are pressured by deadlines and often have to scramble to fit things into a schedule that might already be extremely busy.

In our career example, let's say you need to take a few classes in order to get your certification or license. That is not a big deal as each class takes only a week to complete and they are scheduled every month. So two classes will take you two weeks to complete. Again, that is no big deal.

So you see your boss is likely to retire in two years so you figure you have two years to get those classes completed. Since this is basketball season, you figure you'll take those classes in the fall when there are no games scheduled. So instead of getting those classes done now, you put them off for several months.

But next month your boss gets a promotion, hits the lottery or just retires early because he got a nice inheritance and he no longer needs to work. You apply for his job but guess what? You don't have the license or certification and there is no way you can get it in time because this month's classes are full and interviews are set for next week!

Or, and this happens all the time, the same job in another company opens up and you want to apply for it. But you don't have the qualifications and even if you make it to the interview stage, you are likely to get passed over for the person who has the education and certification or license!

The end result is that you lost out on a great opportunity and that opportunity might not come around again for 5, 10, 20 or more years if the person that just got the job loves it and stays in it until they retire!

This happens far more often than most of us realize. People who are pro-active and do what they can now to prepare themselves for later will find themselves more prepared for what comes their way than everyone else.

They will be able to take advantage of more opportunities, have more data and other information available to them when they need it, and will be able to respond faster and more accurately when required to.

Inability to See the Future

One of the best reasons to become pro-active and take care of things now rather than later is because we never know what is going to happen tomorrow let alone a month or more from now. Things always seem to happen at the worst possible time and that can throw even the most carefully planned day into turmoil.

How many times have you set aside an hour or two to do something only to have an emergency come up that takes up all that time and more?

How many times have you been given a deadline only to have someone tell you they need that information NOW rather than next week?

How many times have you forgotten about something that was assigned to you or that you knew about over a month ago?

Have you even had all the good intentions of doing something only to wake up sick as a dog or had to tend to someone else who was sick and that prevented you from doing what you wanted to do?

All of these situations happen to everyone sooner or later.

There is absolutely no way we can know what is going to happen tomorrow no matter how smart we are or how good our intentions might be. If you think you are different, then think again. If you absolutely, positively know what is going to happen tomorrow I suggest you invest in the stock market today!

Being pro-active means doing today those things you can do today. It means taking care of things you are aware of as soon as you have the time to do them. If you have a free hour today, get something done even if it isn't due until next week because you might not have that hour next week!

If you know your computer is acting strange, do your back-up today instead of next week because your hard drive might crash tomorrow and all your files will be lost. In this case, a little bit of pro-active action will save a ton of time and work in the future.

How Does This Relate to Career Advancement or Growth?

Hopefully now you have more than a good idea why it is so important for people to adopt a pro-active attitude when it comes to both their professional and private lives. So now let's take a look at how this will also help us in our efforts to either start, maintain or grow our career.

First of all, pro-active people tend to produce at a higher level than those who are reactive. They tend to get more done in less time and usually produce better quality work as well. So you could say that pro-active people are the perfect trifecta when it comes to performance. More work, less time and better quality. All of these traits are appreciated and in demand by employers in any industry or size business.

In addition, pro-active people tend to have the information they need when they need it. That means being able to act faster and with greater accuracy. That means having the information to write the best possible resume as soon as they need it. It means having the qualifications to take advantage of any situation that comes across their lives.

Last, but certainly not least, they stand a much better chance of having their skills up to date. They usually will be pro-active in updating skills, taking classes to learn new skills and keeping up with industry trends and information through reading and attending seminars.

Pro-active people are also usually in demand because they address issues before they become problems. Or they address problems when they are small and resolve them before they become major headaches.

People who have a history of this are also in demand by employers and Human Resources professionals.

Being able to bring your accomplishments like these up in an interview will help you as well.

But the most important benefit to advancing your career is understanding that knowing what you need now and getting those things done will enable you to take advantage of opportunities that come your way.

Pro-active people understand the value in planning ahead and being prepared. Much of what we discuss in this book involves being pro-active. Planning out your career and knowing what you next steps are is being pro-active. Knowing what is needed to get to the next step and getting those things done now is being pro-active.

Keeping yourself 2 or 3 steps ahead in life will enable you to maintain better control over your destiny. Being in control will enable you to move forward in the direction you want to move in with fewer mistakes and setbacks. Being in control also saves you time and resources and most of all stress.

Stress is something that is part of everyone's life. For those looking to advance or change their careers, stress often plays a major role throughout the process. You will encounter much less stress if you know moving forward that you have done everything you need to in order to prepare yourself for the next step. You will be more relaxed because you know you have done your best and that you have prepared yourself for what likely is coming next.

Last, but certainly not least, think about this for a moment:

There are bound to be failures in life. No one succeeds all the time and no one is perfect. But it is a lot easier to accept failure and learn from it when you know deep down in your heart that you did everything possible to help you succeed. Most of us can live with failure if we know we did everything we could to prevent it.

But when we fail because we were lazy, or because we didn't do something we knew we should have done, that is something different. That is something we may carry with us for years until we recover from that error. Sometimes we might never recover. That is very hard to accept.

So from this point on, in order to have more control over your career and other parts of your life, let's adopt a pro-active attitude. And let's do that today and not put it off until tomorrow!

Go the Extra Mile!

One good thing when it comes to looking for a new or better job is that it is easy to look better than most of the other applicants. This is not due to any magic formula or special things you can do. But there is one thing you can do that will set up head and shoulders against most of the other candidates.

That special something is going the extra mile or making the little extra effort that most people refuse to do.

Do you realize the amount of success you can experience if you are willing to do the things that others are not willing to do?

Do you realize the opportunities that are sitting out there waiting for people because others are not willing to do the work or whatever is required of them?

Even more to the point of career advancement, do you know how many opportunities are lost because people do not do the extra work other people are willing to do?????

Look, a lot of people in this world today are just plain lazy. They do not do what they should be doing to grow their careers, to bring them success and to maximize their earning potential. We have people out there who will not take a job they feel is beneath them and we have people who will not take the time to perfect their resumes, learn about the companies they are interviewing with or upgrade their skills!

I guess you can say there are a ton of people out there who feel just being good enough is good enough for them! That is an extremely dangerous attitude to have. Why? Because once you get that attitude, you stop trying to improve and better yourself. You stop trying to do something better and you stop learning more in the process.

I have a friend who was unemployed for quite a while. He was offered a job but he turned it down. Why? Because it paid less than what he made before! He said he was worth more than that and it was beneath him to work for less money! Meanwhile he was bringing in NOTHING while he was out of work!

Then we have people at work who feel that certain tasks are either beneath them or not worth their time. Those tasks are left to others and guess what? THOSE people become the "go to" people and they get all the exposure!

But all of this is not about taking a minimum wage job or doing demeaning tasks or anything like that.

What it is about is sitting down and determining what it is that you need to do in order to get what you want in life and then doing it!

If doing something nobody else is willing to do will advance your position in the eyes of your boss, then DO IT!

If you are offered a job that will help support your family and it pays lower than you are accustomed to, TAKE IT and look for something else in the meantime!

If there is something you can do better or more thoroughly than someone else, then PUT IN THE EXTRA EFFORT!

If you look at the life stories of some of the most successful people in this world you will see that most of them did some pretty nasty things in their early days. They did all those things not because they enjoyed doing them but because they saw those tasks as a means to make their lives better!

Our ego's often get in the way of doing what we should in life. We feel we deserve better and refuse to do certain tasks we feel are below our level. But someone else is there and willing to do them and they wind up with the opportunities down the road.

We all see the person at work who always volunteers for projects and responsibilities while others go home at 5PM. We see some people coming in early and staying late while other people watch the clock. The funny thing is that when the people who put in the extra time and effort are rewarded, the other people wonder why!

You need to make a decision on how you are going to approach your career and your life in general. Are you going to be the one who puts in the extra effort or are you going to be in the other group who do only what they feel they need to do in order to get by?

Are you going to be the one who will go over their resume for the 15th time looking for little things you might do to make it better and more impressive? Or are you going to be the one who throws a decent looking resume together, quickly proof reads it and says it's good enough?

Are you going to be the person who says "I'm not being paid to do that?" or are you going to be the person who sees an opportunity or a way to get something done and grabs it?

Are you going to be the person who gives up or are you going to be the one who sticks to something until they are successful?

At this point you have a choice. You can follow the lead of successful people and do the very best job you can even if it means spending more time, asking for more work or doing a better job than anyone else. You can choose what type of person you are and which road you want to travel down. But there is one thing that might make all of this a moot point.

With that in mind, I have one more question I would like to ask you:

Do you take pride in your work and what you do?

I ask you that because if you take pride in everything you do it is far more likely that you will be willing to do whatever it takes to do things right. You will put in the extra time because you know the results will be better.

You will volunteer for more work or do the things others won't because you see the value and you take pride in your job, your efforts and a job well done. It will make no difference that you are doing more than everyone else because it is the right thing to do.

These are exactly the things that others don't bother to do and that leaves the doors wide open for you to walk right on through. Those are the doors that open up opportunity and success for those who work hard and do the right thing. So open those doors and take advantage of what lies behind them!

Volunteer

Have you ever noticed that there are always people around who seem to always volunteer their time, skills or expertise in order to solve a problem or make something better? These are the people who always seem willing to roll up their sleeves and get to work.

Then there are the other people who just dive in and do things they know have to get done without even waiting to be asked. They just see something and they take care of it. They don't look for credit or recognition; they just take care of things.

This is exactly the way you should be if you are looking to get ahead in your company or elsewhere. There are a few important reasons to adopt this particular attitude. Even if your motivation is totally selfish in nature, volunteering will pay off for you!

Think about what happens when you volunteer your time and services. Other people benefit because you solved a problem or helped create something that might have otherwise never been created. You benefit because you have experienced something new and probably increased your knowledge at the same time. It is a true win-win solution!

People who know you will think more highly of you and your bosses or your company management will see you more favorably as well. They want people who will dig in and solve problems or help the company achieve a common goal. They don't want people who sit back while others do all the work. In other words they want you!

When it comes to getting a new or better job, what you have done in your currently job, or any experience you had in the past will be of great benefit for you. If you have volunteered in any capacity that will look extremely good on any resume. You can cite specific examples of how you volunteered to solve a problem and how successful you were.

Volunteering takes initiative and interviewers and management look for that in people they plan to hire. If you can show a history and being one of the first people to step up and solve a problem or create something that is very desirable to potential employers.

Always remember that very often the difference between the person that got the job and the runner-up is very small. It might come down to a single bit of experience or a single entry on a resume. Education is sometimes equal and experience can be comparable. So it comes down to who has done the most or accomplished the most.

So if you can add something positive to your resume, or have specifics to add to your responses in an interview that might be all you need to swing that job offer over to you. Never underestimate the power of showing you are one of the people who step up and take charge. Almost everyone looks for that in a prospective new hire!

Work on Those Communication Skills

One of the most valuable skills anyone could possibly have is often completely overlooked by most people. Those skills are your communication skills. Now communication means more than just talking to someone. Communication skills encompass the entire communication process from speaking to listening and everything in between. Communication is far more than just talking.

Communication skills are what we use to let others know what we are thinking, what we want them to do or to convey information we want them to know. If we communicate effectively we leave no doubt as to what we are saying and what we mean. People have a clear understanding of what you said, what you meant and what you need.

That means that very little is left to chance and the results is that as everything is more easily understood, fewer mistakes are made. Things get done right the first time which means more gets done in less time with fewer mistakes and usually for less cost.

Unfortunately, some people have poor communication skills and cannot effectively let others know what they are thinking. They leave areas of confusion and doubt in the minds of others and often leave them to figure out what they heard. They sometimes are required to connect the dots and hope they connect them properly.

When this happens, and people are not sure about what they heard or the meaning behind it, confusion sets in, poor judgments and decisions are made and the result is that more mistakes are made, time is wasted and more resources are used.

For example, you need a task done at work and you describe it accurately and in such a way that the other people know exactly what you want, chances are pretty good they will move in the right direction and do it right the first time. They might have questions along the way but they will proceed in the direction you intended.

But if you communicate poorly and people misunderstand what you want, they can move in the opposite direction thinking that this is what you want rather than what you intended.

All the work they do will be for nothing and sometimes that work will have to be "undone" before things can get back to normal.

In the context of career advancement and job hunting, communication skills are critical in several areas. You need to be able to convert your experience, skills and attributes into words and place those words in the proper manner into your resume. If you communicate this information clearly, your resume will be effective. If you communicate this information poorly, your resume will lack impact and will probably wind up in the trash bin or in a folder no one will ever open again.

If you go into an interview and are able to talk articulately and put your thoughts into words effectively, people will listen. If you can communicate your strengths and suitability for the position effectively people will see you as a viable candidate. If you fail to get the other people to understand what you bring to the table you will be seen as a poor candidate.

But communication skills involve more than just talking and listening. There are many things that make up the communication process. While we cannot go into each one in depth, here are the main areas that you should be aware of.

If you desire any in-depth knowledge on any one aspect, we suggest you either take a course on communication skills or read a good book about it. There is far too much information that we could possibly fit into these pages!

Before we get started, there is one thing we need everyone to understand when it comes to communication. Only about 7% of what we communicate to others actually comes from the words we use. The other 93% comes from our tone of voice, our emotions, body language and other non-verbal factors.

So communicating is more than words. Listening is more than words. You need to take everything into consideration to properly understand not only what is being said but why it is being said. If you cannot do that, you are not likely to be communicating effectively.

Please stop for a moment and think about what we just said. Think about how emotions can effect what we hear and the meaning behind it. Think about examples where you knew emotions were causing people to say something they really didn't mean. Think about how anger can alter the words we use and the force behind them. Truly understand this before continuing.

Now we will cover some of the main points you should know about and understand regarding communication skills:

Using the Right Words

Even though the actual words we use when talking may account for only 7% of the content, the choice of words is still very important. The better the choice of words the more accurate we can convey our thoughts and intentions.

We should use words that are easy to understand so that more people will be able to figure out what we are saying. It does not good to use complicated or unusual words to describe common things. When we do that we limit our audience and increase the chances of being misunderstood. So if a 2 or 3 syllable word will accurately describe something, then use that word and not an 8 eight syllable equivalent.

You should also choose the appropriate words for the setting of the conversation and the people you are talking to. For example, if you are in the bar with friends you might use so-called "common language" between each other because there is a certain level of closeness between you. But you should not use that type of language during an interview. As the saying goes, "If you are not sure, don't say anything to anyone you wouldn't say if your grandmother were standing there."

Thinking before Speaking

Oh, how we really wish at times that we had just waited a moment or two before blurting out something we wish we could take back. It is amazing how many people speak before they actually think about what it is they want to say and how to best say it!

Interviews are the best example of thinking before you speak. One should always wait a beat or two after being asked a question so that you can think things through a bit and use the proper words. Most often when you do give even a second or two thought you change something to make your words better and more accurate.

Always give yourself the chance to think about what you are going to say before you say it. You cannot take back the words once they leave your lips. You open yourself to criticism, hurt feeling, misunderstanding and confusion whenever you talk first and think second. This might take a bit of practice but train yourself to think first and speak second. This practice will never let you down.

Learning to Really Listen

It makes sense to understand that if words make up about 7% of what we are saying then we are not really listening all that well if we just hear the words. IN order to listen effectively to have to "hear" everything.

You need to hear the words, the emotions behind them, and the gestures and body language of the person speaking. Only when you take in all of these components can you truly be listening effectively.

One particular problem people have with listening is that they are thinking about what they intend to say next while the other person or people are speaking. So at least part of our brain is being used to think about which words we want to use instead of listening to what is being said. Despite our brains being the marvels that they are, when they are otherwise occupied something is bound to be lost. Comprehension is usually the first thing to go!

Don't Interrupt

One very important communicating skill is letting other people talk. We have become so fast paced these days that we try and rush through everything and try and get things done as quickly as possible. As a result, we sometimes hurry things so much that things get lost in the process.

Interrupting people while they are talking carries a few dangers with it. First, interrupting people stops the free flow of information and you might not get the benefit of hearing everything the person has to say. You may think you know but until you get all the information you may never know the full story or the truth.

The other thing that letting people talk helps accomplish is letting people tell their story and vent their emotions. Sometimes just the process of telling people something helps them calm down and become less angry. Since calm people tend to communicate better and more accurately than angry people, it is best to let them talk and let them calm themselves down.

Staying Positive

The human brain is an amazing thing and it reacts in strange ways at times. One of those strange ways is how it sometimes reacts to negative words or phrases. When the human brain hears a negative word, it sometimes equates that with the feeling that it is not getting something it wants or needs. The brain shuts down and doesn't really process the words that follow the negative word.

That is why it is critical that we stay away from negative words and phrases like "can't" "won't" and "shouldn't" because we want to keep the brain engaged so the flow of information will remain uninterrupted. For example instead of saying "I can't do that" we might say "What I can do is...." That second statement is positive in nature and most people would want to hear what is being said next because that is what they are going to get. The negative response might have the brain shut down so it can create its own angry response!

In an interview setting, every response you make should be positive. Do not dwell on the negative. If something negative is brought up do your best to turn your response into something positive that came out of that situation. This allows the overall mood to be positive and upbeat instead of negative and strained. Remember, you want to create a positive impression and the words you use will go a long way in making that happen.

Emotions

Every word we say is influenced by the emotions that are present when we utter those words. Angry or excited people tend to communicate much less effectively than calm people do. That is because emotions override common sense and our ability to control and filter the words we use and how we use them.

Even more important, when we are angry or upset, our brains spend more time thinking about what we are going to say next than listening to what we are being told. We lose focus and our ability to truly concentrate. In fact, angry people sometimes convince themselves that things are not going to go the way they want even though they actually might be. They come looking for and expecting a fight and that is not good!

When you are trying to communicate with an angry or emotional person, you should first attempt to reassure the person and get them to calm down. This will not happen all at once. You will have to do this slowly with each statement or action making the other person calmer and calmer. When they are calm enough you will be able to communicate more effectively.

While you are not likely to get involved with angry people during the job hunting process, sometimes interviews will try to get you out of your "comfort zone" by asking difficult questions and even being slightly antagonistic. When this happens, it is especially important that you keep calm and in control at all costs. The purpose of this type of interview is to see how you act and respond under pressure or stress. Though not a common interview practice, it could happen depending on the type of position you are interviewing for.

Body Language

Body language is the term used to describe the physical characteristics we employ when communicating with people. This includes facial expressions, body position and stance, movements and any other physical indications someone might give during the conversation.

You can tell from a facial expression whether someone is happy or angry. You can tell by the way someone sits whether they are comfortable or nervous.

How far or close someone positions themselves to you might also be an indication of how they feel about you at that particular time.

It is important to be able to observe and recognize these things when you communicate with people. These indications can give you a very accurate indication of the direction the conversation is going. You might be able to tell is someone likes what you are saying or not or whether you are making them happy or upset. If you get indications that things are not going the way you want them to go, the earlier you notice that the faster you can change your approach or your words. That makes it easier to hopefully get things back on track.

For example, in an interview setting if the interviewer frowns during an answer, they might not be happy or pleased with your response. If you notice that you might try and add to it or take things in a different direction. Being able to notice little things like emotions and body language just make it easier to communicate more effectively.

It is important to understand that while all parties involved in the conversation carry the responsibility of listening and talking properly everyone needs to try their best to make sure everyone understands what is being said.

But in an interview, YOU must assume ALL that responsibility because YOU are the one who needs to be understood properly!

If the interviewer misinterprets what you said, or if he gets the wrong impression about you, it matters little to them. After all, there are more applicants out there waiting. But it is you that wants or needs the job.

While this is not necessarily fair, in this particular setting, you have the most invested in the process. So make every effort to arrive at the interview early so you will not be stressed or tense and give yourself time to calm down before going into the interview.

Once you are in the interview, choose your words and responses carefully. EVERYTHING you say should be said in such a way that it makes you appear better in the eyes and ears of the interviewer.

Use positive words and make all your responses positive in nature. If you must discuss something negative make sure you point out something positive in the outcome. People love when other people can take a negative situation and turn it into something positive.

Be friendly and personable but not too familiar. Remember this is a business setting so communicate appropriately suing the right words and the right type of language. It might be fine for the interviewer to speak one way but you should stick to speaking and acting in a professional manner at all times.

Most of all just learn to be aware of what is going on around you. Know and understand the feelings and emotions of those you are talking to. Try and notice if they are impressed or unsure of you and then take action to change that attitude. These are the little things you can do to help set you above the other applicants. Just one little thing can make all the difference.

Thinking Outside the Box

Unfortunately for some of us, life doesn't come with an all encompassing instruction manual. We need to be able to think on our feet and make decisions as we go. Though this can be difficult and stressful at times, it is what makes so much of life special and rewarding. Unfortunately it can also cause us to hold back and act safe or maybe even not act at all.

The ability to analyze a situation and come up with new, different or innovative resolutions is a wonderful ability to possess and one that is in great demand by virtually every company or organization. This is often referred to as "thinking outside the box". That means not allowing yourself to be constrained by only doing what has always been done before.

Perhaps the best example of thinking outside the box would be an inventor.

That is the person who sees a need for something and then goes about inventing something to address that need. In most cases that means creating something that has never been created before.

For hundreds of year people sat in the dark or read by candlelight until Thomas Edison invented the electric light bulb. Marconi invented a way for sound to be transmitted through the air and brought us the radio. Philo Farnsworth brought us the television and that changed our lives forever as well. Imagine how different life would be without those three inventions?

For us, the ability to think outside the box might mean looking at a problem at work and coming up with a better way of handling it. It might mean discovering a different way of doing things in the warehouse that cuts down on the time needed to ship out packages. Or maybe a change in work flow to make things faster, easier or cheaper.

Those things might seem trivial in nature when compared to inventing the light bulb or television but the same thought process and attitude was used in all those examples. That attitude is the attitude that something can always be made better or that there is more than one way to solve a problem.

People who possess this skill are respected by others and well thought of in their company and industry.

Management loves problem solvers and pioneers because that is how change occurs and advances are made. If everyone accepted things as they are and made no attempt to better anything, we would all be stuck in the same world our parents and their parents lived in.

As far as career advancement is concerned, people who think outside the box will be in greater demand because their abilities and attitudes mean improved operations, better products, more advancements and higher profits for the company. Anyone who can bring that to a company is bound to be in demand!

Ask yourself if you are that type of person. Are you the one who sees something and wonders how it could be made better? Or are you the person who just accepts things the way they are and moves on? If you are the latter person, you need to re-evaluate the way you look at things. Start looking for ways to make things better and act on them. Learn from your mistakes and refine your approach.

Document your successes and become the person known for their unique approaches and frequent success. Do not be reckless but do not be inhibited either. Sometimes sharing ideas is enough to make a change really happen. You might not know how to build the machinery or change a layout or procedure but suggesting that to someone who does know how can be just as important.

If you are looking to advance within your own company, having a track record of being an innovator and someone who is always looking to make something better will serve you well. Managers who look into the future and see change before it hits are extremely valuable. People who are able to see the value in a new product or identify a particular need for a certain product or service can create huge profits for their company.

If you can walk into an interview and have examples where you saw a need or a problem and came up with an innovative solution will often make an interviewer stop dead in their tracks and take notice. That is because today a lot of people do not want to go the extra mile or make the extra effort. They also do not want to subject themselves to the possibility of failure either. In other words, they want to play it safe. When you play it safe, you often miss out on the full benefits available to you.

As you go through your career look for ways to do something different that will improve something in your life or environment. Don't limit yourself to what everyone else says is the only way to do something. Explore new things. Try out new ideas. Be innovative.

Take this to another level by becoming a leader. Become someone who is not afraid to take charge and lead people in the effort of getting something done or achieving a certain goal.

Don't be afraid to lead people down a different path if you believe that is the best way to go.

Keep in mind that everything around you was the result of someone seeing a need or having an idea for making life better. Every piece of equipment was designed because someone saw a way to do something faster, better or more accurate. That little music player sitting in the palm of your hand is there because someone years ago hated that cassette tape player that was big and bulky and could only hold 20 songs if you were lucky!

If you are trying to advance your career you can do so only by increasing your perceived value to others. One of the best ways to be able to do that is by creating the perception that you are an innovator and free thinker that believes in change and always looking for ways to make things better.

If that's not you, then you should make it you.

Self Promotion

This might open more than a few eyes but it's time we come to grips with something very important. You can have the best education, possess the very best skills, and have more achievements than most everyone else in this world and it won't do you one bit of good if no one knows about it. Being anonymous is good when you give to charity or help someone in need but it does you a disservice when it comes to advancing your career or your standing in your industry.

Self promotion has a certain stigma about it in our society but that is mostly because it has received a bad name because of a few shameless and obnoxious people who constantly brag about who they are and what they have done. You know the type. The co-worker who constantly brags about his latest accomplishment or your brother-in-law who constantly tells you how great he is and how much money he has. No one likes people like that.

But real self-promotion does not have to be done in an obnoxious manner. You don't have to run to your boss every time you have a good idea and you don't have to write a memo taking credit for your last success either. But you do need to take credit or make others aware that you have done certain things or accomplished certain tasks. The key is in how you go about it.

You should be doing this in an indirect manner that is not perceived as bragging or "sucking up" to anyone. Just saying something to your boss like, "My idea for streamlining the office workflow is working out very well. It cut down processing time by 30%!" is all you need to say to let them know it was your idea and not someone else's. Plus, you should do it in private and not in a meeting or public setting.

Another example might be letting someone know you finished your college degree. You might give your boss a note asking him how to update your Human Resource profile to include your new degree. This makes him or her aware that you now have your degree without you appearing to brag about it to anyone.

The sad part about things today is that if you do something great and no one knows about it you may get passed over for that promotion that was just posted.

You might be the person who likes to just take care of things without the recognition.

But when the promotion goes to the person who does less than you but let's everyone know about it, that won't make you feel good either.

It is a fine balance but you need to do at least a little self-promotion in order to advance yourself in the workplace. Without it you might find yourself stuck right where you are.

When it comes to looking outside your organization, self-promotion starts with your cover letter and your resume. It continues right straight through your interviews and follow-ups as well. In fact, your self-promotion should not stop until you have the position in hand and all your compensation and benefits have been negotiated!

As we have said before, the job hunting process is one of competition. There will be other people applying for and competing for the same job. Everyone is going to try and make themselves appear to be the very best person for the job. They are going to promote themselves in any way they can. Or at least they should.

This is not the time to be shy or modest. This is the time where you gather everything you have done or accomplished in life and find the best way to make yourself look like the perfect candidate. Other candidates are doing this so it is in your best interest to do so as well if you want to land the job offer!

Your cover letter and resume are your sales letters. In those pages you should be promoting yourself as a well qualified and impressive individual worthy of additional consideration in an interview. Your entire focus at this point should be on creating a perception that you MUST be brought in for an interview. Not that you might or should be brought in, but that you MUST!

In your interview you should use that opportunity to promote what you have done or accomplished and show how all of that will help you in the position you are interviewing for. Your goal should not be to create the impression that you are a good candidate for the job. Your goal should be to create the impression that you are THE candidate for the job. The only way you can accomplish this is to promote yourself effectively!

Do not expect people to know what you have done even if you are interviewing within your own company. If you have done something impress that is relevant to the job you are applying for it is your obligation to yourself to make everyone aware of that. Not in an obnoxious way or by being boastful but by making them aware in a nice way.

You accomplish that speaking in a confident manner and delivering the information in an excited manner.

For example, if the interviewer tells you that one of your responsibilities if you are hired would be to manager some remote staff in other locations, you might reply in a semi-excited manner, "That's great! In my current job I manage 14 remote employees and our group has made out sales targets for the last 8 years. In fact, last year our group won the award for highest productivity. I was very proud of that!"

In that one statement you let them know several things. First, you have direct experience that is relevant to the position. Second, you were successful at it over a long period of time. Third, you and your group performed so well you won a performance based award. You did all this without bragging or being obnoxious! You just stated facts and were excited in doing it!

The best way to prepare for applying for a job and promoting yourself is to have a list of accomplishments and qualifications and then picking from that list the most impressive and relevant items. You would then work them into your cover letter to create more interest.

For your interview pick the most relevant and impressive examples and work them into your responses to questions. Knowing in advance those things you want to bring up will make it easier to include them. Remember, preparation is everything! If you know in advance what you need to say you will be less likely to forget something!

In your follow-up letters or e-mails promote yourself a little bit more by restating your specific experience and drawing the lines between your experience and the job and how you feel you are the best candidate.

There is one very important part of self promotion that you need to be aware of. It only works well when you appear confident in doing it. If you appear meek or unsure of yourself when talking about yourself, it might not work all that well. You need to believe in yourself and what you have done. You have to appear confident in your belief that you are the best candidate for the job.

Don't be afraid to talk about yourself. It might not feel comfortable but you need to do it. Not only in interviews and on your resumes but whenever you are talking to your boss or others above you in the company. Don't let others take credit for your work or accomplishments. And don't let others promote themselves while you remain in the background. If you have done something good, you should get the credit for you.

If done correctly, self promotion will help make others aware of just how important you are and how worthy you are of their attention and consideration. When you really think about it, isn't that the entire purpose of the entire process?

To make others aware of how great you are and why they should hire you. Looking at it that way, not only should you promote yourself, it is expected that you will! After all, that's you job at this point!

So just go out there and do your job!

Developing Relationships

If you read just one chapter in this book, let it be this one. That is because a large number of jobs are landed not through answering ads or submitting resumes but because of personal recommendations or through relationships with people in their home town or industry. Forming relationships will help you not only get the inside track on certain opportunities having someone personally recommend you to others will give you an advantage over strangers who apply for the same position.

One problem employers have today is that it costs them a lot of money and resources to hire someone new and train them to become proficient in the job they were hired for. This takes not only time, but money as well. If they spend the time and resources developing someone who turns out to be a great fit that is great. No one will mind spending that time and resources for someone who turns out to be an asset to the company.

But what if the company spends all that time and effort and the new employee turns out to be a complete failure or someone who was not what they thought they were? Not only have they lost all that time and spent all those resources, but they now have to start all over again and spend time and resources on the hiring process as well. It is conceivable that a year or more might be lost when the wrong employee is hired for some positions!

It is for this same reason that employers often make applicant go through several interviews, personality tests, background checks and other steps before an offer of employment is extended. It is not because employers wish to be difficult with their applicants but instead because it is so important to target the right individual for the position.

Another problem employers suffer with is that many applicants will go to great lengths to portray themselves as the perfect d=candidate for the job even though that might not be the case. Following the steps and tips outlined in this book will help any applicant portray themselves in the best possible light and many applicants will do just that.

But another group of applicants will formulate a resume based not on fact and truth but instead on giving the employer exactly what they want whether that be factual or not.

This does not mean they stretch the truth; they manufacture something and present it as the truth. There is a huge difference.

So in many cases the employer hires what they think is the perfect candidate only to find our weeks or months later that this employee is not what they expected when they hired him or her. This can happen even when backgrounds are checked and interviews have been completed. Talking about doing something is a lot different than doing it on a daily basis! So the company now has to start the process all over again.

I give you all of this background not to give you ideas or discourage you but to make you aware of just why a personal recommendation can be a powerful friend to you when it comes time to landing a job. Stop and think for a moment on just why that is the case.

If someone is going to recommend you for a job, he or she will do that at the risk of possibly devaluing their reputation. For example, if I work for a company and I tell them that Jeff is a great guy and a wonderful worker and that they should hire new for the new manager position, if they do hire him and Jeff is a complete loser it will not reflect well on the person who recommends them.

So it stands to reason that a personal recommendation from someone they respect or admire will give them a much greater chance of hiring the right person for the job.

That is compared to choosing someone based on a resume and an hour or so of face to face conversation. You should never underestimate the power of a personal recommendation!

This is also the reason many positions are filled without ever even being posted or advertised. Applicants are identified through personal connections and interviewed without the position every being announced to the general public! This happens far more often than you might ever think!

So now that we understand why personal contacts are so important, let's talk about how to go about networking and building the relationships that might be of use to you in the future. We should say up front that this should not be the only reason you establish these relationships. You should be looking for a mutually beneficial relationship and not just befriending someone so that you can use them. When people start relationships for that reason it is usually obvious to others what is really going on.

There are several ways to build a network of individuals that can mutually help each other in their careers. Here are just a few of the people you might seek out:

Management in Your Existing Company

If there is a way to increase your visibility within your own company, try and take advantage of it.

Volunteer your time and expertise in company sponsored events or activities. Participate in events that bring you in contact with management above you in a social setting where they can get to know you outside of work.

Volunteer for special projects where you will have a chance to work with people above you in the company. This is where you can show them first-hand what skills you possess and the attitude you have towards your job and the company.

Do not be concerned with getting out the door on time and be more aware of things you can do to make yourself better known and more respected. This will pay you benefits further down the road.

Participating in Focus Groups or Peer Groups

If there are focus groups or local groups pertaining to your industry or job function join them. Participate in the activities and get to know other people in your town or area that work in the same industry. You never know when you might hear of an opportunity in another company.

Local trade associations are a great way of getting more involved and better known within your industry. Many of your skills and most of your knowledge will be directly transferrable making you an attractive applicant even when you are not looking!

Your focus when joining these groups should be to increase your visibility while helping out the organization and those within it. This is not something to go to just to walk in and hand out business cards. You are there to establish yourself and get to know people in your industry or occupation and hopefully do some good at the same time.

Joining Industry Organizations

Just about every industry has an association of some type that holds conferences and meetings throughout the year. Join these groups and become active in them. Volunteer your skills and knowledge to help further industry causes and needs. By doing so you will not only build valuable contacts but also get to travel to some nice locations at the company's expense!

Joining Local Organizations

There are plenty of organizations like the Boy Scouts or Girl Scouts, Habitat for Humanity and other similar organizations where you can do some good for other people and meet new people at the same time.

Though these people might not be in your industry, you never know who you might meet and who those people might know either.

Sometimes opportunities come to people through people their friends and associates might know. So just because someone you know is not active in your industry does not mean they don't know someone who is!

Again, your focus should be on furthering the causes of the organizations you join and everything else will fall in line. The more you put yourself out there, the more visibility you will get to all kinds of people. The experience you get might also make a fine entry on your resume as well.

Volunteerism

Any time you can volunteer to help an organization or group of people you will get to meet different people from all walks of life. You never know who these people will be or what they might be able to do for you. But no matter what may happen, you will still get to meet new people while helping others at the same time!

Become a Mentor

Mentoring is one of the finest things a person can do. To be able to help someone else by sharing your skills and expertise is a very rewarding and fulfilling experience. You never know what will come from such an arrangement. Sometimes the student winds up being the master!

In its most basic form, networking means putting yourself out there so that you are among people who can help you further your career. Most of the time this will be at work related seminars, meeting and other events but the same thing can happen anywhere.

Always be on the lookout for someone that you think might be good to know. Cultivate the relationship and make people aware of who you are and what you do. Volunteer your expertise to help solve a problem or accomplish a goal. Even though you are not likely to be compensated for your time and efforts, you will build relationship after relationship which will tend to serve you well in the years ahead.

I cannot stress enough that you must not approach networking as something that is one sided where people help you and you do nothing in return. The best relationships are formed when you help others and help them solve problems or make something better.

When you demonstrate your value both as a person and as a worker, you open people's eyes and make them see you as someone who might be a good fit working with them or someone they know. Their high regard for you and what you do will be the main reason why they will place their reputation on the line when they recommend you.

It should also be mentioned that networking is not something that is done for 20 minutes and then you are done. Networking is a constant activity that carries on month after month and year after year. You will be building these relationships slowly over time not all at once. So approach things with the right attitude and be sincere in what you do and why you are doing it. Place your needs behind the needs of others and you will find your advancing your own cause and career at the same time without knowing it!

Keep Learning

Part of establishing or improving a career means getting a new or better job. In order to accomplish this, a person must represent themselves as a person of significant value to the company that they are interviewing for. Put in simpler terms, the company must be impressed by who you are and what you have to offer.

Unfortunately for some of us, the skills we once learned that enabled us to succeed reasonably well are probably at least partially outdated. The world is constantly changing and not much is the same as it was last year if not the same as it was 10 or 20 years ago. Since everything had changed, it makes sense that what we learned in school is now no longer up to date or complete.

While most people understand this, many of us fail to keep our knowledge and education up to date and because of this we find our knowledge and skill sets well behind recent graduates. Even though we have more experience, our level of knowledge will usually fall short.

If you are in the latter parts of your career this might not be a problem or issue for you. If you are doing quite well and only have a couple of years before retirement, the investment in updating your education might not be worth the benefit. But if you have 10, 20, 30 or more years ahead of you, it might be worth your while to develop a plan for improving your education and keeping your skills up to date. If you have just graduated and think this does not apply to you, please continue reading as we will get to your situation as well.

The best way to get your skills and knowledge current is to develop a plan where you constantly update your skills in small increments either my taking seminars, attending conferences, reading trade publications or books or getting on the job training through your company or trade association.

The benefits of doing this are that you not only keep your skills up to date but your work and performance will continuously benefit because you will always have up to date skills. There will be few times when you will be forced to handle current tasks with outdated skills. You will be able to do more in less time with better results if you have current skills.

Another benefit is that you will always be marketable and you will always be ready to take advantage of any opportunity that might come your way.

If you wait until your skills are significantly behind and then find yourself with an opportunity that requires higher level skills, you may fall short of the other candidates and miss out on what might have been a career changing move.

Another benefit is that continuously updating your skills requires less time and effort than it does to go back to school and take classes all over again. You can read a book in your spare time. You can take a seminar in one day or attend a conference in a day or two. Those events can be spaced out so the workload is spread out and will more easily fit into your schedule. In other words, you can keep you skills current much easier when you do not allow yourself to fall too far behind.

But if you have let your skills and knowledge erode or fall far behind, there are things you can and should do to reverse that trend.

First of all, take action now before you fall further behind. Do not wait another week or month to get started. Even if you just start reading a book or schedule a seminar or class, take steps to get started now! No matter how little you start with, you will still be further ahead than if you did nothing!

Second, develop a plan on how to get your skills back to where they need to be. Research available classes or other resources and determine how you can work them into your schedule.

There will likely be fees involved and your budget will likely be a consideration as well. But keep in mind that your education is an investment and that money spent improving or increasing your knowledge will pay you back for years later.

Third, after you create a plan, assign some deadlines to each step and try and hold yourself to them. Move steadily towards your end goal. Take classes or read regularly. Identify the most needed skills and get those first and then move on to other skills. Do not allow yourself to get distracted. Remain focused until you have reached your objective.

Last, but certainly not least, we do not want to fall back into how we were before and start to let our new skill level decline like we did before. Commit to constantly learning new skills and keeping your education up to date. Monitor yourself monthly or quarterly and ask yourself what you have done to keep you skills current or add new ones since your last review.

These types of reviews are important because they allow you a way to make sure you are still moving in the right direction. They let you identify problems or lapses before they become problems. This kind of internal feedback will help keep you on the right path and heading in the right direction.

Now, here are some things you should NOT do:

You should not wait until you need updated skills to go out and get them. Not only is it more time consuming and difficult to do so in this manner, it will take time that you might not have to get the skills you need to take advantage of a certain opportunity. Always do what you can to be ready for anything that might come across your path.

Do NOT wait to be told that you need to update your skills! If you wait until someone tells you, that means your skills have eroded to the point where someone else has noticed a decline in the quality of your work. This not only leaves you vulnerable to losing your current job but it makes you look irresponsible at the same time.

Do NOT tell yourself that your skills are good enough for two reasons. First, unless you got out of school within the last 6 months or so you have new things to learn. Everything changes quickly today and even the textbooks you used in school are probably a few years old anyway!

Second, if you tell yourself that being good enough is good enough for you, then you have other problems that are probably hurting your chances of getting that new and better job. You should always strive to be more than good enough. You should strive to be the best and most qualified person you can possibly be. If you are at your best and give your best and someone else gets the job, then good for that other person.

But if you are just good enough and lose out to another person, then shame on you. Expect more of yourself. Expect to be one of the best, not one of the rest.

Do NOT feel you are too far behind and that things are too hopeless. See a career counselor or visit a local employment office to see what options are available for you. It is never too late to learn and it is never too late to get better at something. Take baby steps with your skills. Update them from poor to good, then from good to better and finally from better to best.

Do NOT allow money to be your excuse. You can take out books from the library. You can take adult education classes or classes from your local employment offices. There are government programs you can use and sometimes there are even programs available through your employer that will help you get the education and skills you need.

As far as your career advancement and job hunting are concerned, you want to be proud of your education whether it be formal education or on the job training. Do not hesitate to bring up to the interviewer that you constantly update your knowledge and skills so that you are always capable of performing at your highest level.

Make them aware of the classes, seminars, conferences and other educational things you have taken or done over the last year or two to show them you are committed to excellence and not just getting by. Believe me when I tell you that companies and interviewers look for signs that people take their skills and performance seriously. They look for people who act pro-actively and do things because they want to not because they have to.

The last thing you want is to be asked about your education and have to reply that you don't know something or have to promise to get that particular education if you get the job. While that is sometimes out of your control, you want to enter that interview with as much education, experience and confidence possible.

You want to be the person who can stand with the best when it comes to every part of their background and skills sets. You don't want to be the one who has to play catch-up or try to explain away a deficit of any kind. This is a competition and the person who is the most prepared and the most impressive will win almost every time!

Developing a Great Reputation

If someone were to ask your co-workers, friends or relatives what they thought about you, what would they say? Would the responses be overwhelming positive? Would they be very critical or negative? Or would they be mixed and kind of non-committal? Or might they say nothing at all?

Contrary to what some people think, how others look at us and feel about us will have a considerable effect on whether we are successful in our career advancement or even obtaining that important first job.

While there are some people who move through life not caring what others think of them, they often fail to understand that how far they go, or even where they go, is influenced by how they are perceived by others. No one goes through life totally on their own without help or interaction with others. They might think they do but they don't.

A positive opinion about you in the eyes of others will make people value your presence in their lives and your contributions to it as well. A negative opinion brings the exact opposite response. If people feel negatively about you they will tend to stay away from you, avoid you when they see you and resist your efforts to interact with them.

So I hope we can agree that how others feel about us will have an impact on how we live our lives as well. As far as our career is concerned, how others feel about us is very important. In some situations those opinions and feeling can be critical to our success.

That is why our reputation in the marketplace and with others needs to be the very best we can possibly make it. We need to create the perception that we are a valuable part of the company and that our work and other contributions are valuable as well.

We need to do this so others will either recommend us for opportunities that come up or that others who have heard of us will think of us for those same opportunities. Much of the success people have in life came from being a good person and having someone else help them get a new job or a better job. They do that because the other person was known as a good person and an asset to the company.

But how do we go about creating a good reputation? Well the answer to that question is easy but the process often is not!

Your reputation is built over time through the way we act, how we go about performing certain tasks and also by our values, morals and personality. Each one of those factors plays an important role in our reputation.

People with good reputations are usually known for being hard workers, dependable, honest, trustworthy, caring, innovative, and have an overall good attitude towards most things in life. Because of those attributes these are the people who are usually sought out by others in both business and social settings. In other words, these are the people other people want to be around. These are the people others think very highly of.

That is exactly what you want to be in the eyes of others to position yourself for the greatest shot at success.

People with bad reputations, however, exhibit the opposite in life. They are known for being lazy, they are not reliable, they tend to remain in the background and do as little as possible, and they lie, cheat or even steal, and have an overall negative attitude towards others in their life. In other words, these are the people we avoid in life. These are the people our parents told us to stay away from because being associated with those people can be bad for our reputation.

This is exactly what you want to avoid when it comes to being seen by others.

If you are seen in this light by other people you will almost be guaranteed failure or a lack of success in life.

So reputations are built over the years. If we want to be seen in a positive way by other people we need to exhibit the qualities that other people respect and admire. That means helping others, becoming known as a good resource, volunteering for additional work, being ready to help even when it isn't your particular job to do so and willingly sharing ideas and thoughts even when you won't be getting the credit. It means taking an interest in other people and not always thinking of just yourself or doing things that benefit others and not just yourself either.

It also means being honest and forthright and not taking advantage of others or taking credit for things you didn't do. It means doing what you said you were going to do and be able to be counted on when the need arises. Perhaps the most important, it means treating other people with dignity and respect regardless of how they treat you.

If all of that seems like a lot of work, that's because it is. But every single one of those items are things that you SHOULD be doing as a matter of course. You should treat people well and you should be someone who can be counted upon. Most of all, you should always be honest, upfront, and behave in an acceptable manner.

That should not be work for you. Those things should be done without thought and effort. They should be habits for a good person.

Take a long look at all of those elements and see how many of them you already do on a daily basis. Chances are you already have many of those items in your personality and life already. Maybe you fall short on one or two but that is fine. You can always change the little things and change the perception others have of you.

If you are lacking in almost all of them, or a few of the really important ones, you are going to have to first overcome the negative feelings people already have of you and replace those feelings with positive ones. That means making a strong effort to be the person others are drawn to. Offer to help out more, ask people for a second or third chance to prove yourself. If you have hurt someone or done something very wrong, be the one to apologize and ask for forgiveness. But most of all, exhibit the new and better behavior at every opportunity you possibly can. It is going to take some time to get people to change their opinions of you and to overcome the suspicion that remains for a while but it can be done.

There is saying that goes something like, "It takes years to build a great reputation and minutes to ruin it."

That means once you have created a great reputation you have to be careful not to do anything to damage it. Even one mistake can set your reputation back years and create doubt where there was none before.

For example, if you take credit for the work of someone else, or if you lie in order to get something you didn't deserve, your reputation will suffer. If you steal or take something that isn't yours and you are caught, people will be suspicious of you for a long time afterwards. Possibly forever. If something goes missing in the future you might be the one they look at first. All because of something you did a while back.

Your reputation should be treated like gold. It follows you throughout your life and has a direct impact on how your life proceeds and whether you will be successful or not. You must take every effort to protect it and guard it. That means keeping your distance from people who less than stellar reputations and it means refraining from trying to take the easy way out.

Now that we understand the value of having a great reputation, here are a few things you can do to enhance your reputation or rehabilitate an existing one:

Start Behaving Properly

Always behave professional and properly.

Don't do anything you wouldn't do if your spouse or grandmother were standing there with you. That means using proper language and behaving in a way that is respected by others. Be a good person at every opportunity.

Start Treating Others Better

People deserve to be treated with dignity and respect. That holds true even if they are not treating you in that same manner. Always take the high road and treat people right no matter what they do to you. Never lower yourself to their level.

Ask for More Work

Be the one who always is willing to do more than their fair share. Even if that means you are taken advantage of by some people. Be the one others learn to depend on for help or input. This will serve you well at the same it is making others stop and take notice of you and what you bring to the table.

Ask to Help

Don't wait for someone to ask you for help, reach out to them and offer it. Let it be known that you are always available to help anyone when needed. This alone will be appreciated by just about everyone and will help change their perception of you quickly.

Just make sure you help for the right reasons and not just to steal credit from someone else because you helped them.

Volunteer Your Time

Volunteer in your community. Offer your time and services to worthy organizations. Spend a day building with Habitat for Humanity or volunteer to staff a blood drive. Help the Boy /scouts or Girl Scouts. If you have a particularly valuable skill or experience, become a mentor and teach it to someone else. In other words, get involved and help others.

Be a Positive Influence

No one likes a person who complains all the time or acts like the world is coming to an end. Instead, they like the person who remains upbeat even when the you know what hits the fan. Adopt a positive attitude and demonstrate that every day. Let the little stuff roll off your back. Make other people happier by acting happier around them. Trust me, it can be infectious.

Look for Ways to Help Others

If you see something you can do to make something easier or better, do it. If you see a way to make someone else look better, then do it. If you see an opportunity to help someone else, take advantage of it.

Be Pro-Active

Don't wait until someone tells you or asks you to do something. If you see a need or if you notice something that should be done, just go ahead and act upon it.

Always be Honest and Ethical

Always take the high road and keep everything honest and ethical. Tell the truth, don't lie, cheat or steal, and don't take credit for the work of others. Conform to the ethics of your industry and situations and always, without exception, do what is right. If there is any doubt, act on the safe side and always do the right thing at the right time. This is absolutely critical. Once you do some wrong or illegal it can follow you for the rest of your life!

Don't Take Advantage of Others

There will always be situations where other people might be vulnerable or weaker than usual. Don't be the person who swoops in to take advantage of that weakness. Instead, be the one who comes in and helps them get through it. Be the one who watches over things and protects them from others if they can't protect themselves. This is a powerful way of establishing friends and relationships with others.

I hope after reading this chapter that you are now aware, if you weren't before, of just how important your reputation really is.

Your reputation surrounds you and extends further out that you might imagine. Your reputation precedes you and people will often hear about you before they actually meet you.

So it just makes sense to create a powerful impression right off the bat by creating the very best reputation you possibly can. Yes, it takes work and it takes commitment but if you do it and do it right, the rest of life will become much easier.

It's just the right thing and the smart thing to do.

Learn How to Write

Writing is one of those skills we never really think about. We were taught how to physically write in elementary school and some of us never developed that particular skill any further. Some of us took writing classes in high school and college but we never really practiced those skills much after the class was done and we got our final grade.

But writing is a critical skill for everyone to have. The way we write provides a glimpse of who we are and how well we are able to communicate in life. If we write well we can get our point across effectively and possibly even in an enjoyable manner. If we write poorly, our thoughts might become garbled or unclear and we become boring to read as well.

When it comes to our career and business life, writing takes on another level of meaning. We might be called upon to write presentations, memos, letter, reports, even an article a manual or two.

Whatever we are called upon to do, we have to know how to write well in order to product a quality result.

Writing is also an important part of our career growth and job hunting process as well. Throughout the process we are going to be called upon to write our resume, a cover letter or two as well as any follow-up communications we need to send. While it is possible to have a professional design and write our resume and perhaps a cover letter, we cannot expect a professional to write every follow-up letter or other document for us. We really need to develop writing skills for that task and more.

You basically have three goals when it comes to wring anything. You first goal is to get your ideas and thoughts across to the reader in a clear and concise manner. That means writing in an easy to understand format and using words that are easily understood by the vast majority of people likely to read your letter. It also means not taking 14 pages to deliver 2 pages of content.

Your second goal is to make your document easy and enjoyable to read. Your document should not be difficult to read or understand and the reader should find it easy to follow and enjoyable to read. It should follow a logical progression that leads the reader to the desired conclusion.

The third goal is to have the reader actually read your document though to the very end.

This is accomplished by combining goals one and two to create something that is not too long, is easy and enjoyable to read and makes it easy for the reader to understand and follow what you have written.

For our particular purpose that means writing a well thought out and to the point cover letter and an informative and information packed resume. It means writing a well designed follow-up letter that highlights your strong points as well as other information you feel is relevant that has not be brought up yet. And it means doing all of this in as short and concise manner as possible. In simple terms, no 4 page rambling cover letter, no 3 page resumes filled with misspellings and grammar errors, and no poorly written follow-up letters either!

To help you sharpen your writing skills, here are a few things you should consider and some tips to improve your writing style and help you get your point across to everyone:

Write to Your Audience

It helps to understand who is going to be reading your document before you write it. If you know who is going to read it, you can tailor your writing style to that particular audience. For example, you would use a different style and wording writing a children's book than you would if you were writing to an adult audience.

Always keep your intended audience in mind when choosing the type of words as well. Write so that the vast majority of people in your targeted audience will be able to easily understand what you have written and can follow it with little or no effort.

Understand Your Purpose for Writing

Everything we write has a purpose behind writing it. No one writes something just because they like writing. You are either looking to convey a thought or idea to someone else, inform someone about something, write a story, entertain someone, or whatever particular purpose/reason you might have.

It is important to understand what your purpose is before you start writing so you can make sure that by the time you are finished you have fulfilled that purpose in the best possible way.

For example, if you are writing a cover letter, your purpose is to get someone to read your resume and invite you in for an interview. So your writing style should be one that makes you look the best that you can be and makes you appear to be the most impressive candidate.

When you right something and then go back over it when you are finished, you should always ask yourself if the final document achieves or fulfills the original purpose you had for writing it. If it does, that's great! If it doesn't, or it doesn't do it well, then either start over or make chances until it does.

Use an Appropriate Style

The type of document and application also has an impact on how you write it and what style you would use. For example, you might inject a bit of humor into an article on dating and people might find that amusing and enjoyable. But if you were writing an article on death or funerals, humor is not likely to be appropriate or amusing.

You also want to avoid boring people to death as well. If you are writing a technical publication of some kind then you can be more dry and technical and still maintain the interest of your audience. But if you are writing an article intended for the general public or non-technical people, the dry approach might bore your audience to tears!

Be Respectful

Always write using words that are not likely to offend anyone reading your document. Stay away from off color or vulgar language unless it is 100% critical to the point of the document. The same goes for off color jokes or comments concerning things where people are easily offended.

For example, some people have strong feelings regarding religion, sex and other topics. Unless your subject has a direct relationship to any of those areas, keep your opinions and feelings to yourself. You do not want to alienate any part of your audience.

Don't Get Fancy

Keep in mind that the people who read your writing will tend to have very different level of education. Some will have grade school educations while others might have a Doctorate. You should write to the lower education level so that everyone will be able to understand what you are writing about. The exception to this might be if you are writing something specifically for a certain group of people who are likely to have a certain level of education. If that is the case then write to that level.

Writing to the lower level is not meant to offend anyone or put anyone down. Our focus is on making sure everyone can understand what we are writing and not judging people based on their education.

That means using words that are easily understood over a wide range of people and educational levels. In other words, if a 2 syllable word will convey exactly what you want then there is no need to use an 8 syllable word instead. Long and fancy words make things more difficult to read and even more difficult to understand. If you have to stop to think about what a certain word means, you should think about using another word instead!

Write to maintain a certain flow and make it easy and enjoyable for the reader to read what you have written.

This increases the odds that they will remain engaged and actually read everything all the way through until the end.

Don't Get Technical

One mistake a lot of writers make is using a lot of technical words or jargon that only people in a certain industry or job would understand. The rest of the people become lost because they have no idea what certain words mean. This is an example of writing to your audience.

If you can explain a technical concept using non-technical words then you should choose that style and manner of writing. If you must use technical words in your writing make sure you take the time to explain what the word means to your audience. This way you are educating them at the same time you are explaining something to them.

Create Interest from the Start

Unless you are writing the great American novel and need to set up the background for a storyline, keep your writing short and to the point. Most people want to read about something and enjoy reading the content but if you take too long to capture their interest, they will stop reading and move on to the next chapter, book or article.

You might just have a few moments to convince the reader to keep reading. That is why "setting the hook" with interesting and relevant content from the beginning is the best way to keep the reader interested. Your title or opening paragraph should create interest and make the reader want to read more. Without interest most people will just quickly scan over what you have written and they might not even do that!

Keep this in mind as you write your cover letters and resumes. In those documents you MUST create and maintain interest or no one will read them all the way through.

Keep it Short & Sweet

If you can write what you need to write in 2 pages and deliver all the content you need to within that space, then don't take 4 pages to accomplish the same goal. For most people, reading is something they do to get information or for enjoyment. A novel might be 400 pages if it is well written but your note or cover letter should be one page.

Keep in mind that your resume or cover letter is not the only one that one person is assigned to read. They might have 10 or 100 of them to read so they don't have a lot of time to spend on each one. If they open your envelope and there is a 4 page cover letter listing everything you want them to know, they are not likely to read it at all because they just don't have the time!

Pick out the most important highlights and keep the letter to one page and the resume to two pages at the most. You might have to leave an entry or two off the resume but you will greatly improve the chances that it is read all the way through!

Make it Easy to Read

Whenever you write anything, make sure that it is easy to read. If you use a word processor and a computer, don't use a 6PT font that requires a magnifying glass to read. Make it 10pt or larger but not so large that it appears overpowering.

Make sure everything is aligned properly and that it looks professional and neat. If someone sees a sloppy layout they might not even bother to read it. The content and how it looks are a direct reflection on whoever wrote it. If you are not sure of how your resume or cover letter should look, get a book on resumes or search online for some examples.

If you are physically wring something by hand, and sometimes we still do that, take care to make sure your handwriting is easy to read. Do not write quickly and illegibly so that people cannot read what you have written.

If your penmanship is poor then consider either practicing to write more clearly or take lessons to correct your flaws.

Any time we write something that no one can easily read we open the possibility of misunderstanding or confusion. If you have to, print instead of using cursive or script. This can make it easier to read.

Write with Depth & Flair

Anything we write should create and maintain interest. It should also get our point across and in some cases, appear impressive to the reader. Always understand the reason for writing what you are writing and then choose the best words to get your point across for that purpose.

For example, when writing a resume, your purpose is to look good and sound impressive. So if you achieved your sales goals for the last 5 years, you could write "Met sales goals for last 5 years" or you could write "Exceeded assigned sales goals for the last 5 years" or " Exceeded sales goals by over 10% on average over the last 5 years and led my division in sales during that time period."

The first entry sounds kind of dry and dull. It doesn't create much of a picture in the mind of the reader. The second entry adds the word "exceeded" which sounds more impressive and makes a better impression. The last entry adds a specific number which makes the statement clearer and gives it more "punch". It will create the most powerful impression in the mind of the reader.

Just be careful that in your attempt to create a more powerful and vivid impression that you do so without lying or creating false statements. If you didn't exceed your goal by 10% don't say you did. Be honest but make everything you put in your resume or on your cover letter look more impressive by using more descriptive words and phrases.

The purpose of any piece of writing is to create a mental picture of what you want to convey through your writing. Choosing the best words and phrasing help you create that picture exactly the way you want people to see it.

Create a Flow

All good writers will tell you that your writing should have a certain flow in it. That means your writing should follow a certain pattern that is organized and leads the writer in a certain way from the start of the document through to the end.

In a novel the storyline takes you from the beginning of the story through to the end giving you information and events as you need them for the story to develop. You would not talk about a character without first introducing them to the reader. Nor would you refer to an event that has not already happened in the story.

In your resume and cover letters, you should be organized as well.

Your letter and resume should tell a story about who you are, what you have done, and where you want to go in your career. That is the flow and the flow should be organized and focused. It should not jump around from one thing to another and back again.

Sometimes it is helpful to first create an outline listing everything you want to include in your letter or resume and then checking things off as you write. This helps you stay focused and also insures that you do not leave anything out as well.

As you proof read what you have written, make sure it follows a logical progression and that everything is presented in an orderly fashion that is fluid and easy to understand.

Don't Assume

One common mistake some people make is assuming the reader has specific knowledge of what they are writing about. They might take for granted that the reader knows what an industry or technical term means when they might not. That can lead to confusion, misinterpretation or cause them to abandon reading altogether.

That is why it is important to make sure to use words that are easy to understand and to stay away from anything that the reader may not be familiar with. If you must use a certain word or term, make sure to explain it within the article or document.

This can prove difficult when space is limited as in a cover letter or resume. If possible, save the technical entries and information for the interview where you will have the time and ability to explain things and give background where required.

Remember to also write to your audience and their particular background. When you are able to do that you may be able to make certain assumptions about their level of understanding. The same goes for writing to specific people that you know. But when you are righting to unknown individuals don't automatically assume they know what you are writing about. Be careful, be specific and explain things where necessary.

Proof Read

Whenever you right something, be sure to red back over it a few times to make sure that everything is exactly the way you intended it to be. You want to make sure there are no grammar errors, spelling mistakes, formatting issues and content issues as well.

You want to make sure your words and phrases accurately convey what you intended in your writing. Did you "paint" the right picture in the mind of the reader? Does it flow well? Is it complete? Is it easy to read? These are just a few of the questions the writer needs to ask before calling everything complete.

One trick writer's often use to catch spelling errors is to read the document in reverse. This way nothing will flow and you will not finding yourself reading the sentence instead of looking at each word for spelling errors.

Some other tricks for proof reading are to read what you have written aloud to hear how it sounds and flows or print it out and mark up the document for any corrections or underline it as you read it.

But there are two other ways that might be much more effective for you. The first is to have someone else read what you have written and give their own evaluation. Because they have not seen it before, their minds will not assume what is written is correct and they will be more open minded when it comes to evaluation. When you read it you may tend to skim over it rather than really reading it.

Last but not least, it makes sense to wait a period of time before proof reading something you just wrote. If possible wait a few hours or the next day and refer back to what you wrote and re-read it them. Your mind will have been "purged" of what you wrote and you will be able to read it with much more of an open mind.

One word of caution: Spell check is a great friend when writing on word processors. Use it first to catch the high level mistakes but always do a manual read as well. Spell check does NOT catch everything!

If you are sending out a small document such as a cover letter or resume, it takes just a few minutes to manually read and scan through it to make sure. Always remember everything you write reflects about you so take every step to make sure it is accurate and what you wanted to write in the first place!

Become the Big Kahuna!

The best and sometimes easiest way to get a new or better job or to take your career to the next level is to have people come to you instead of you seeking them. This can be accomplished by creating an image and reputation as someone who is at the top of their game and well known within the industry.

In every industry there are people who are well known as the leader and shakers in that industry. These are the people who have had significant success or are well known as authorities in that particular topic or industry. These are the people you see on television, hear on radio, or seen speaking at or giving lectures to their peers.

Though you might not think so, all of these people started their careers at the same place you did. They started at or near the bottom and they worked their way up to where they are now by doing several different things.

You can accomplish the same things in your career as well as long as you are willing to do the same type of things they did.

We will show you the types of things you can do to create this type of image. There are several things you can do but they all share one common theme. They all are designed to get you exposure and get you known in your respective field. That is how you get people to recognize you and make your name come up whenever certain opportunities are discussed.

Doing these things will also make it easier for you to get considered for positions that you seek out as well. It stands to reason that if you are well known when someone sees your name on a resume it will spark recognition and your resume will stand out from the rest. So don't think doing these things are only for the movers and shakers because they are for everyone! Besides, who says you can't become a mover and shaker anyway?

Here are a few things you can do to get to be known as an authority in your industry:

Lecture

If you want to get exposure as an expert in your field, offer your services as a guest lecturer or speaker at local events, presentations and other opportunities in your area or even at the National Level.

People see speakers and lecturers as experts in their field even though they might not be any more qualified than you or I.

Every time you do lecture or present, make a note of it and start forming a list. Bring this list with you on interviews or mention a date or two in your cover letter especially if the event was within the area of the company you are submitting to. Remember, anything that makes you appear better or more qualified should be promoted!

Another benefit of lecturing is that the people who come to listen are usually people in your industry and chances are you will meet some influential people and make connections that may help you in the future!

Teach

If you are really an expert in your field, why not take the opportunity to hold a class or teach a class at your local university or school? Every student is a potential contact and every class is an entry on your list and resume!

Write a Book

Writing a book is a great way to become known as an authority in your field of expertise. It sometimes doesn't even have to be a popular book! Just having it available or known or on your resume might give you instant credibility!

Write an Article

Articles in trade publications are a great way of getting your name out to the public. Thousands of people read these publications and having your name associated with your industry is always a good thing.

As with writing any kind of article or book, make sure it is well written, accurate and factual. Your name is associated with it so be careful what you release.

Create a Blog or Website

Today the internet and blogging is one way to get a lot of exposure for next to no cost and very little inconvenience. You can host your own website for a few dollars a year and there is software available for a low cost that will easily allow you to create and run your own site or blog. This can help you develop a following and get your name known as someone who is a valued expert and resource in their field.

This may also show up during internet searches giving you even more credibility!

Be a Guest Commentator

Depending on your particular career or area of expertise, there might be opportunities out there for guest commentators or panelists at trade shows, conferences, rallies or other venues.

These help get your name and image out to the public and you never know who might see or hear about your appearance.

Volunteer

Volunteer your time and services at local events and through industry organizations. Local industry groups often hold meetings to advance the industry and your presence at these meetings can help you establish friendships and relationships that might lead to opportunities down the road.

These are among the easiest ways to develop your initial presence in the area or industry. Starting small will give you the experience and credentials to work up to larger and more prestigious events. Always consider that whenever you think these small meetings might not be worth your time. Everyone has to start somewhere.

Become a Spokesman

If there is a product, service or organization you are particular proud of, consider offering your services as a spokesman. If the product and service are really good and have a great reputation, connecting your name and image to it can be very beneficial. Of course, the opposite is also true so be careful what and who you support.

Become an Advocate

Some careers and industries need advocates to help further that particular cause. Advocates are personal spokesman and supporters who are will to support, speak or act to further the cause of the organization. If this is something that you feel might interest you, look for qualified groups or causes in your area and check them out to see if they are a good fit for you.

Work Trade Shows

Many companies participate in trade shows throughout the country and the world. Some people love to work the booths while others just hate it. It is not glamorous and can be tedious but you can meet some influential people and if you interact well with people you might make some great impressions during the show.

Whatever avenue you decide to take to establish yourself as an expert in your field, keep in mind that you do not do this overnight. It takes time and patience to establish yourself as an expert.

Try and do the things that will help establish you at first and those things that can give you the fastest return on your investment of time.

Whatever you do decide to pursue, it is important that you do it first class and produce a quality effort. Publishing a book is great and today there are places where you can easily self-publish any book for a relatively low cost. But presenting a cheesy and low quality book to someone, or having your name on a low quality piece of garbage, will do you more harm than good.

Always make the effort to produce a high quality result. Treat your name and reputation like gold and never do anything that will harm it. Your reputation can either be a great help or a huge hindrance to you. You have to decide which one it will be by your efforts.

Be a Positive Force

This chapter will be a quick hitter because this concept is very easy to understand and very basic. People look for positive people to hire for jobs within their company. They do not want people who will come in and dwell on what's wrong and have a negative outlook on things. If that is you then you are going to have trouble getting any job let alone a better one!

The world is full of complainers and people who sit back and let everyone know what's wrong yet do nothing to make anything better. That is not what good employees or desirable people do. Companies look for people who can spot things that are wrong and then go about making them better. They are not looking for complainers; they are looking for the people who can be counted upon to do something about it!

They want people who look at things positively and take proper action.

With that in mind here are a few attitude related things you should work on or at least become aware of when it comes to going after your next job or improve your reputation in your current one:

Eliminate Negative Words & Attitude

If you are the type of person that always sees the negative in something, or that dwells on only the negative parts, you will need to change your attitude moving forward. You will need to start trying to find or look for the good in things or for ways to make things better.

When you are confronted with something that doesn't work, try to figure out why and see what can be done to make it better. When you have a difficult time dealing with someo0ne, try and find good points about that person as well. This may help you alter your approach.

A great way to start to change is by eliminating the negative words we use from our vocabulary. Words like can't, won't and shouldn't should o longer be used by us. We should substitute phrases like "what we can do" for "we can't do that" and other similar changes to turn negative comments into positive ones.

Don't Complain or Find Fault

If you want to turn off people, just complain about everything or everyone.

Tell them how bad it was then, how it is no better now and everything that your company is doing wrong and how you are powerless to make things any different.

In an interview, if you want to turn off the interviewers almost immediately, tell them how your last job or your current job was so bad and how incompetent your co-workers were. Tell them about all the stuff was wrong and how you are trying so hard to get out to someplace where things are done right.

This type of behavior does not send up a red flag, it sends up an entire red fireworks display that says "Don't hire this applicant whatever you do!"

Don't Bad Mouth People

There is a saying that goes "If you can't say something nice, don't say nothing at all." That is extremely true when talking about other people both in and outside the interview setting. People who constantly talk about other people and all their faults are usually those with faults of their own or the person has extremely low self esteem.

Good people do not talk bad about someone unless there is a valid reason to do so. If someone is placing the welfare of someone else in danger, or if their performance is sabotaging the project then perhaps something needs to be said in private.

But in the office or during an interview, do not use the opportunity to bad mouth someone else even if that person is another candidate for the same position. Defer from making negative comments even if directly asked. Doing so shows class and self-confidence. Your refusal to make yourself look better at the expense of someone else will reflect very positively on you.

Another way of looking at this might be to put yourself in the interviewer's shoes. Would you want to hire someone who talks bad about others? Once that person works for your company, don't you think they would talk bad about you and others within your company? That alone is often a big enough reason to pass over an otherwise well qualified candidate.

Offer Solutions

The reality of life is that there are always negative situations and negative people that are part of those situations. So you cannot escape negativity you have to learn how to deal with it. You don't deal with problems by complaining about them. You deal with problems by analyzing them, discovering what is wrong and then taking steps to make things better.

Part of job interviews usually have a negative question or two to see how the candidate responds.

They might ask you to talk about a negative situation you had to deal with and how you handled it. When they ask this question they are looking for a few things.

First they want to see how you reacted. Did you react by complaining or giving up or did you do something about the problem and made an attempt to resolve it? What you did and how you reacted is important to know about prospective applicants.

They are also curious about how you went about changing something. Did you involve others or did you work alone? How did you overcome an obstacle that was standing in your path? Did you eliminate the obstacle or did you get creative and figure out a way around it?

All of this points towards your ability to create solutions to common and not so common problems. They want to see how you react to negativity and whether you are the person who tends to add to the negativity or reduce it.

This may sound like a minor thing but how you react is one way to see inside someone to discover what their real attitude towards things really is. This is one way people find to look inside and see what's really there.

It can take a while to change your approach and attitudes towards problems and negativity. You should consider this a work in progress and you should start addressing things in a pro-active manner.

That means starting today and making constant practice.

As we stated, first try and eliminate those negative words. Then force yourself to find at least one or two positive things in any negative situation. Train yourself to look for solutions instead of just complaining. You might even want to take a previous problem and rethink how your response could have been different or more positive.

Whatever you decide to do, just make sure it will help you think and act in a more positive manner. This is the way change happens. It happens by a change in attitude and behavior that is practiced until it becomes a habit.

Be Organized

Although you might not think so, being organized is an important part of your career advancement strategy. This is because organization skills will help you not only in your current job by increasing your productivity but they will also help you get and stay focused on what's important when you are job hunting.

The purpose of this book is to give you not just a good chance at success but the very best possible chance of success in landing the job and the career you want. Because of that we also include "off topics" that while not directly associated with getting a new job none the less still play a significant role in that process.

As far as career advancement is concerned, being organized will help you be better able to keep track of information, have the information more readily available to you when you need it and will also help you avoid losing valuable time and resources in the process.

Keep in mind that every minute or hour you spend looking for something you know you have, that means there is less time left to do other things. It might sound like a trivial issue but sometimes it can make the difference between success and failure.

Now that we hopefully agree that being organized has its benefits, here are a few things to help you get stated becoming more organized not only in your career but also in life in general:

Create a System

Behind every method of organizing something there is a system. A system means determining how you are going to categorize your information, documents and other things so you will know how to find them and use them.

You might decide to store your documents in a folder, in a separate storage box or container or even store them digitally on your computer. You might keep track of things in a notebook or on your computer as well. It is not important right now HOW or WHERE you do it, just that you start doing it!

Create a separate file folder for your resumes. Have another folder with copies of cover letters you have sent. Also have a master list with the dates you sent your resume and where it was sent to. It is also useful to keep copies of ads you responded to in case you need to refer back to them later.

Define a Place

All the organization in the world will not do you any good if you can't find something when you need it. If you have your boxes and folders and documents all over the place, even if they are organized you will still have to remember where each one is.

Through you probably will have several documents concerning your job hunting process; they should fit in one or two boxes so it is best to store everything in one area or location. Use file folders to keep like documents together and make everything easier to find. If you also store things on your computer, open ONE file folder, label it clearly and then use sub folders to store other documents.

If you do not keep everything in one location, or make them easy to find you could spend hours looking for something placed in a pile of papers in another room or wherever that might be. If everything is placed in one or two boxes, at least all you have to do is search through that one box!

The same goes for computer docs or scanned docs. Keep them stored in one folder! Do not have them stored individually all over your hard drive. If something also pertains to something else on your computer, store the document in both places so you will always be able to find it regardless of where you need it.

Reduce Clutter

Clutter is responsible for most lost time and lost items than most any other bad habit. If every folder is chocked full or your file cabinet is bursting at the seams, that's because you either have too little storage space or too many documents!

Clutter even makes it difficult to store things where you might want them. If you always keep your documents in one drawer but that drawer if full now, you might be tempted to store them someplace else "for now" and then file them properly later. The problem with that is that "later" never really comes and things are spread out all over the place.

Another reason clutter is counter-productive is that even when something is in the right place if it is under a pile of 47 other things you sometimes don't see it or pass over it while you are looking.

Schedule a Purge

Contrary to some people's beliefs, there is no need to save that resume you used 35 years ago when you graduated college unless it has emotional value to you. Even in that case you don't need all 28 copies. One should suffice.

If you applied for a job 3 years ago and never heard back, chances are that cover letter won't be needed any time soon either.

The same goes for any other "ancient history" regarding jobs or opportunities you applied for.

Do a purge of older information at least once a year. You might want to do that right after you land a new job and all the other information becomes irrelevant. You might dispose of it or at least pack it up in one box or large folder and label it for storage.

There is no need to keep phone bills from the 1980's or any of that stuff. Not only does that stuff take up space, it makes it more difficult to find what you are really looking for at that moment. So take the bull by the horns and get rid of some of the clutter in your home or apartment right now!

Job Hunting Information

You should keep records of what jobs you apply for and what is happening with each application. If you apply to just a few jobs, open a folder for each one and place any correspondence pertaining to that job in that folder. That will help you avoid confusion as to which document pertains to which job.

Keep a copy of your original cover letter and the original job ad or posting that you responded to. Having that ad will allow you to refer back at a later date to any specifics that might need to be responded to when going in for your interview.

Depending on the job and the company involved, it might be several months between sending in your resume until you get a response back. Having the ad and everything organized will allow you to refresh your mind about which job was which and what you need to do moving forward.

The same goes for information pertaining to that job. Any subsequent writing or documents should be filed in that folder as well. Include notes from telephone conversations and anything else that might help refresh your memory or allow you to remember a specific name.

After the interview write a summary of important things said during the interview or any other information you feel might be helpful and put that in the folder as well. Many companies will hold more than one interview and having this summary information will help you remember one interview from another and also allow you to follow your notes and follow-up on other things mentioned during the past interview.

Other information you also want to have on hand might be recent income tax forms for proof of salary and employment, copies of certifications or certificates and other proof of education or accomplishment.

The key is to have the information all in one place and readily accessible so you have it right there when you need it. This way you won't have to waste time looking for something when you need it.

It also helps you produce better and more accurate documents as well. When we have information easily available to us we tend to use more of it. If we have to struggle to find it, we might just leave that information out no matter how important it might be. In a process that often hinges on one or two little differences between applicants, that missing data might be extremely important!

These skills are important not only for your career but in the rest of your life as well. Being organized results in getting more accomplished in less time and gives you less stress as well. We have a lot of things taking up our time in life so being organized just makes sense. It's not hard if you create a system and then stick with it!

Conclusion

Well, here we finally are at the end of our journey. I hope you have picked up some valuable and useful information in the process. We did our best to touch on every part of the process to help you not only know what to expect but to get you in the right mood as well.

It is surprising at how many people look at the job hunting process as a random process where it is a little bit of luck combined with education and experience. In reality it is a lot more than that. If you allow luck to play any role whatsoever you are cheating yourself.

I hope you have paid attention and used some of the approaches and techniques we covered in this book to help you design your very best cover letter and resume. We also hope you did your preparation before creating that resume and especially before walking in for your interview. If you did I can guarantee you that you will have a great shot at success than most other people.

Just remember that this entire process deserves your best efforts because you deserve nothing less. I don't care what kind of job or career you have; you should expect the best for yourself. Do not settle for second best or for less than what you feel you deserve. I am not talking about entitlement but rather pursuing your dreams and what you feel you are capable of.

No matter where you go or how well you do, never look back except to see what you did and how you can learn from the results you received. Once you do that, leave the past in the past. Look forward, move forward and demand the best of yourself and for yourself.

You should expect nothing less.

www.ingramcontent.com/pod-product-compliance
Lightning Source LLC
Chambersburg PA
CBHW051643170526
45167CB00001B/306